IDAHO

Missoula

North Fork

Dwor shak Reservoir

Ahsahka

Clearwater

Orofino

Pierce

Lochsa River

Lewiston

Weippe

Kamiah

South Fork

Selway River

TRAFFICKING

A Memoir of an Undercover Game Warden

Tony H. Latham

Epigraph

Defenders of the short-sighted men who in their greed and selfishness will, if permitted, rob our country of half its charm by their reckless extermination of all useful and beautiful wild things...

-THEODORE ROOSEVELT, 1916

Dedication

This book is dedicated to my father, Ken Latham, my
mother, Darlene Latham, and my grandparents, Ardath
and Rulon Henderson, who collectively taught me to
respect the laws of the land and gave me my deep
appreciation for wild critters.

And to Conely Elms and Bill Pogue, who gave it all.

CONTENTS

Preface

Prologue

1 Crossing Paths - 15

2 Mike Best and the Crabtree - 24

3 Into the Clearwater - 37

4 Digging a Hole - 56

5 Back to Uniform - 70

6 Drinking with Charbonneau - 81

7 Steelhead for Porn - 95

8 Loose Lips - 110

9 Indian Time - 123

10 Dying Quivers - 136

11 Burned - 148

12 Going to Church - 160

13 The Heat is On - 177

14 Lewd & Lascivious - 190

15 Breaking Bread - 206

16 Bureaucratic Courage - 219

17 Bear Hunters - 233

18 Missoula Run - 244

19 Buzzguns - 249

20 Imminent Retribution - 263

21 D-Day - 278

Epilogue - 288

Acknowledgments - 300

Preface

The story on these pages is true; it has been sitting in me for two decades wanting out. When I began writing this book, my intent was to identify the guilty using their real names. But when I had the manuscript to its halfway point, I realized it had been my choice to lay *myself* out and maybe it wasn't right for me to violate the privacy of the offenders depicted in these pages—despite their grievous deeds. Thus, the names of the *civilians* in this book are fictional.

The conversations that took place during this investigation with the players were well documented in hundreds of pages of reports. A large part of our speech is executed using vocal inflections and body language that don't translate well when written out. I've taken the liberty of tweaking and expanding conversations within these pages for the sake of clarity and character expansion.

The book is about the criminal trafficking of big game animals in Idaho for profit by immoral killers. It's not about legitimate hunting, so please don't get the two activities mixed up.

Without question, this investigation took my innocence away–it changed me. These events happened in the early part of my career as a conservation officer and forged my philosophy on wildlife law enforcement. My experiences set the foundation for the type of crimes I believe needed vigorous pursuit.

You'll note that I do not use the term "poach." If you ask three Americans what it means, you'll likely get three different answers. The word originated in England to describe the hunting by commoners which was illegal since the king owned all the wildlife. In the United States, the citizens own the wildlife, and thus the old word *poacher* really doesn't work. What fits are words such as *criminal, thief, crook,* and *violator*.

Much of this book revolves around a few Nez Perce Indians killing and selling wildlife to non-Indians and a white man using the Indians to launder his illegal meat. Trafficking in wildlife is a double-sided coin; it takes an illegal market to generate the killing of animals for monetary gain. In this market, *non-Indians* motivated the illegal killing and selling that initiated this investigation.

Wildlife trafficking is a dark part of our country's history; it led to the near extinction of bison and the subsequent conservation movement driven by names such as Teddy Roosevelt and John Muir. This change in direction from conquering to conserving the Wild West resulted in the creation of our nation's first game laws, national parks, and national forests.

It may help the reader to understand a bit about the legal background behind this tale. The Nez Perce signed a treaty with the U.S. Government in 1855 that stated in part: "The right of taking fish, at all usual and accustomed grounds... on open and unclaimed lands." Signing the treaty gave the Nez Perce standing as a sovereign nation and reserved their hunting and fishing rights that they have had since time immemorial. Courts later defined "open and unclaimed lands" to include National Forest lands. As a sovereign nation, the Nez Perce government regulates the hunting and fishing activities of their people. The tribal fish and game code allows their members to hunt big game and fish year-round with no limits or tags in an attempt to maintain their culture. Unfortunately, this liberalization encourages the commercialization of the resource. At the time of this investigation, the following acts were illegal under tribal law:

- hunting with the use of artificial light
- hunting with a motorized vehicle
- selling, bartering, offering, or possessing wildlife for commercialization
- hunting with non-tribal members or allowing non tribal members to assist while hunting

The Nez Perce have their own courts but their apathy about enforcing their fish and game law was a widely-held belief at the time of this story. Tribal members killing or selling wildlife in violation of tribal law *off the reservation* are breaking Idaho State Code 36-504, or as the law states: "It shall be unlawful for any person to import, export, transport, sell, receive, acquire, purchase or possess any wildlife...that is taken [killed], possessed, in violation of any law or regulation of the United States, any Indian law, or regulation, or any law, or regulation of any state other than Idaho." Within this code lies the legal basis for the investigation entwined in this book.

Idaho's Department of Fish and Game is embedded in this story. The view from the trenches, where I was, isn't the same view that headquarters in Boise had. Headquarters dealt with a much bigger statewide picture; I dealt with individual animals and people. Both viewpoints are necessary for the sake of clarity.

I'm proud that I worked for Idaho's wildlife agency and that *I was a game warden*. If I had the opportunity to start all over, I'd do it again in a heartbeat.

Prologue

I was scared. Scared that a late-night deputy would discover the cut lock dangling from its chain on the gate and grab his shotgun. I could almost feel the gun's bore tracking us.

My two companions, Jimmy and Tom, seemed focused, even though they were drunker than hogs. Maybe they had done this kind of thing enough to be easy with it. Maybe it was the booze or the smell of revenge they knew was at hand. But both seemed to have a "don't-give-a-shit" attitude that fed my fear. I feared that lone deputy and I feared my two drunken companions. Jimmy and Tom seemed to be on a mission, and it surely wasn't a mission from God. It was a mission of revenge and greed, and I had fallen right in the middle of it.

I was shaken by how ludicrous my situation was. I was four years into my career as a law enforcement officer and was helping two very drunk tribal members burglarize a tribal church—all while I was on duty. It was simply an insane situation to have gotten myself into. My supervisor knew I was on some "special" assignment and that was all he knew. The case supervisor was seven hours away and assumed he knew what county I was in. My partner knew I had disappeared into the night with my two "pals" who weren't all that enthusiastic about the color of my skin.

And the crazy irony was what I feared most was the muzzle of another lone officer stumbling on three unknown perps in a blackened back alleyway.

Chapter 1

Crossing Paths

I remember the first time I was at Dworshak Dam.
My brother Nick and I were on our way to school at the
University of Idaho in Moscow. He was studying
architecture and I was struggling with a degree in
wildlife management. He wanted to build stuff and I
wanted to be a game warden. Dworshak Dam was being
built and Nick wanted to look at it during its
construction phase. It was no minor project since it
would be the country's third highest dam when it was
completed. It was quite the sight to see.

Twenty years later I returned to that spot near the
dam where my brother and I had looked over its
creation; but this trip wasn't as a curious spectator. I was
recalling the earlier visit with my brother but thinking
about how bizarre this revisit was. I was investigating the
illegal trafficking in wildlife; I wasn't wearing a uniform,
badge, or gun-belt since I was working undercover. I was
about to initiate my first "illegal buy" of wildlife all while
the déjà vu of the past trip with my brother was playing
though my head.

I think most kids ponder what they are going to be
when they grow up. I'm sure I didn't dwell on the
subject, but I do remember my grandmother talking
about her brother Hawley and the respect she had for
him as an Idaho game warden. I don't remember
meeting him until well after he had retired. Regretfully

he passed on before my appointment as an Idaho conservation officer and I never got to talk to him about his career. Hawley Hill attained the rank of Enforcement Bureau Chief, and after I was hired, I found that his troops had called him "Holy Hell" behind his back. It's my belief the nickname came from a combination of fear and respect.

But my grandmother had planted the game warden seed and my mother had reinforced it. I wonder if the two weren't in collusion—the two working off each other like undercover operatives on a sting. The occasional mentions of Hawley and his job made me ponder: *What is this game warden thing all about?*

My earliest memories are riding on top of my dad's decoy pack in the early morning cold while he waded through a marshy swamp to get us to his duck blind called Duck Junction on the Snake River. I'm guessing I was five or six, but it stuck with me; I couldn't wait until I was old enough to carry my own shotgun. Dad raised my brother and me to follow the law. We didn't load the shotguns until legal shooting hours arrived and they were unloaded when the duck regulations said we were done shooting for the day.

The first time I remember being checked by a game warden was with my brother during a duck jump-shooting adventure somewhere north of Idaho Falls. The warden was polite and cordial, and we were legal. I remember name-dropping my great uncle during the contact and recall it getting the warden's attention. At the time I thought Hawley was just another warden; I didn't understand that he would have been this warden's boss's boss at the time of this conversation. And the warden certainly didn't mention Hawley's nickname "Holy Hell" to me.

When I was about seventeen, a warden checked me while I was elk hunting. I hadn't seen any elk, but I'd found a fresh gut pile and head of a spike bull elk lying near a forest road. I mentioned it to the warden, and jeez-louise, it caught his attention. The next thing I knew I was in his pickup truck and he was asking me questions backwards and forwards. The inside of his green four-by-four truck was a well-used semi-orderly office and shop. He had a lidded wooden box on the center of the bench seat acting as a console and desktop. The box was dinged up and looked as if it had been around for a generation. There was a yellow pad clipped to the top of it. A curling photograph of a bloated cow moose was clipped to the left visor. A two-way radio was bolted to his dash with a glowing green light on it. A big black metal flashlight was resting on the dashboard. His truck was like none I had ever seen; it even smelled interesting. And then I looked down and saw his revolver. It was a .357 Magnum, holstered in a leather gun belt wrapped around his four-wheel stick shift. The gun was placed for easy access from the driver's side. I remember asking what it was for, and he looked over at me and said, "There are some bad people out there." This was the first time it sank in that maybe a game warden's job could be dangerous.

Thirteen years after I sat in the warden's truck, a trapper named Claude Dallas was caught red-handed with illegal bobcats by Idaho game wardens Bill Pogue and Conely Elms. Dallas pulled a hidden .357 out and shot both officers down. He then retrieved a .22 rifle from his tent and finished Bill and Conely off with a shot to their heads as if they were animals in his traps.

I never did figure out why the warden was so interested in the spike elk that day. Looking back I *suspect* the elk had been taken illegally during the previous night with a spotlight; perhaps the officer had some knowledge of the crime and was trying to make the case.

When I was hired by Idaho as a conservation officer, my primary responsibility would be uniform patrol and overt investigations, but somehow I was aware that the department conducted undercover investigations. I assumed that I would be briefed on each of these active covert operations. Early in my orientation period myself and the four other rookie game wardens were briefed by the department's head of the Special Investigative Unit. We learned that the "unit" consisted of one full time undercover operative and his multi-hat boss, and that we would only be made aware of any ongoing undercover investigation just before assisting with search warrants or arrests. In short, we were informed that all long-term undercover investigations were on a strict "need to know" basis.

The more I heard about covert investigations, the more fascinated I became. During the briefing, it was mentioned that occasionally patrol officers were recruited to work long-term undercover operations around the state. Another seed was planted.

The five of us rookie game wardens were issued briefcases to carry office supplies in our trucks. Shortly thereafter I confessed to fellow rookie Steve Nadeau that I had set my briefcase combination lock to 0-0-7. Steve smiled and admitted that he had, too. We both got a good laugh out of it.

Game wardens rely on basic police work to solve most wildlife crimes. They get wind of the crime, gather evidence from the scene, and interview potential witnesses or suspects. The biggest challenge in wildlife law enforcement is the frequent lack of witnesses to report the crime, and thus it's often up to the officer to detect it. There have been a handful of academic studies that show less than 5% of wildlife crimes are detected. My experience working undercover makes me believe it's much less. Deer don't call 9-1-1 to report the shooting of a herd-mate in the middle of the night and game wardens don't have a dash mounted radar device to tell them something is illegal. Wardens frequently become creative and rely on covert methods such as using decoys in high crime areas or watching a spot that is vulnerable to wildlife crime from a hidden vantage. Long-term undercover investigations fall into the covert category but are generally conducted as a last resort and only for the most serious criminal activity. These cases usually involve some type of illegal commercialization. For example, there is a great deal of trafficking of golden eagles in North America for the feather trade. A patrolling game warden may detect the killing of eagles by finding feathers, blood and footprints in the snow under a power pole where a bird has been shot. If the officer gets lucky and has the time to dedicate to patrolling the area, he may even catch the shooter with an eagle, but he will not catch the shooter selling a gunny sack of frozen eagles behind a bar at 2:00 a.m. It's frequently the day-to-day game warden patrol, however, that picks up on the possibility of commercialization and passes the information onto the Special Investigations Unit (SIU) headquartered in Boise. The unit examines the information and determines if it warrants a long-term undercover investigation. Analysis of the information includes the damage being done to the resource, the cost of the investigation, officer safety issues and potential for a successful prosecution. Long-term undercover investigations involve a significant commitment of money and resources.

New York City started a "community policing" program in 1990 that was popular with the citizens and had great success in slowing crime down. The program revolved around a tight relationship between officers and the residents of the area where the officers were assigned. Other cities started similar programs but New York City was given credit for the concept. Game departments, however, invented community policing early in the 20th century. All across the nation, state wildlife departments have had their wardens living and working at a community level. The warden gets to know "his people" throughout his patrol area and visa-versa. The officer learns the roads, creeks, wildlife, and hunting and fishing spots used by both the residents and the visitors to the area through day (and night) patrols. Since they can't be everywhere they rely on citizens to keep their ears and eyes open as to who's up to what. The vast majority of people provide information for one reason;

they love wildlife and despise wildlife thieves. People providing information are collectively referred to as "human sources." A few of these sources fall into a second category, I call them snitches. They are the shady types that inform on their fellow crooks for personal gain. If they get the competition out of the way, the informing crook can kill more game. It's this group that usually provides information of commercialization, since the lifestyle of law abiding citizens usually doesn't expose them to wildlife trafficking.

When a warden gets information, the first thing he or she looks at is how the source got the information and why he's coming forth. If the source saw the incident with his or her own eyes, it's more valuable than if the source heard about the incident from a friend of a friend of the shooter's wife. The motive for coming forth must be examined. The motivation is usually out of disgust for what the person did. If the motive smells bad however, the warden has to take the information with a grain of salt. If it turns out the source is coming forth for some indirect personal gain, the information is frequently embellished or may be untrue. No matter the motivation, any information gained must be run through what is called the "intelligence cycle." This process involves analyzing how the information can be verified or expanded. Could there be a crime scene that still has corroborating evidence? Does the officer know of another person that may also have knowledge about the incident or activity? Are there meat locker or taxidermy records that may help? Once the officer has churned the information through the cycle, it is labeled "intel" and a rough plan is developed on what can be done about it. A patrol officer can decide to take the case on himself if he feels he has the time. If it appears that the information can only be properly investigated by a long-term undercover investigation, the officer will have to write it up and pass it on to SIU.

If the information justifies a long-term covert investigation, SIU must decide who is best suited to take the case. For example, if the intel involves somebody selling illegal fur, the investigator must be knowledgeable about the grades and value of fur. If it involves archery, the officer better be an archer. At some point in a developing undercover plan, a "shtick" needs to be developed. The first time I heard this term I thought the investigator was using the word stick. He was a federal agent that had been working a case in the Orofino area some years earlier and was targeting the illegal sale of salmon and steelhead by tribal members. The shtick he used was a mobile jerky sales truck. He told me that after an hour of sitting at his roadside stand attempting to sell jerky, he had multiple offers to purchase wild game meat for processing into jerky. I never did ask him how many salmon and steelhead he purchased, but I'm sure it was a truckload. "Shtick" is an old Yiddish word that means "a devious trick." In the covert world of undercover investigations, the shtick is embedded in the operative's cover. It can be as simple as a reason to meet your target or to be in the area but it has to reflect your investigative goal.

When the information came in from District Conservation Officer Bill Snow that something was afoot at the Crabtree Bed and Breakfast near Orofino, it caused the SIU wheel to start turning. Unfortunately the wheel was a bit squeaky and needed greasing. The previous major undercover investigation had targeted a group of habitual poachers in Southern Idaho. Although it was conducted with due diligence, it finished a mess. I was called to aid in the service of one of three search warrants at the start of the *takedown* (sometimes called the raid phase) of the investigation with several other game wardens. My role was to assist in the service of one of the warrants with three other officers at a residence that possessed the liver from an illegal moose. We seized the liver, gave the occupants a receipt, and listened to their implausible story of how it ended up in their refrigerator. Several months after the raid, I was named in a lawsuit along with the twenty or so officers that had been involved in the case and the suit's list of names went slowly up the chain of command to the director's office. The case withered away in court since it had no truthful basis but it left the department gun-shy of undercover investigations. Even though I'd been named in the suit, I was chomping at the bit for a taste of undercover work.

Chapter 2

Mike Best & the Crabtree

I got home one evening from a patrol and as usual my phone message light was blinking which was a routine part of my life. I had a love-hate relationship with this little electric box since it generally ran my days and nights. I wasn't married and didn't have much of a social life, so I wasn't expecting any of the messages to be from attractive ladies wanting to cook dinner for a hungry bachelor. But this little box had sent me on numerous adventures and it wasn't anything a young game warden could put off. I grabbed my phone log, pulled a pen out of my shirt and pushed the button. First, I jotted down notes from a rancher who needing some help with elk in his alfalfa. Next was the voice of Al Nicholson. As far as I was concerned, Al was one of the finest human beings that ever walked the earth, not to mention that he was a fine game warden who had taught me a bunch. So when Al spoke, I listened. Besides, he was my boss.

"Tony, this is Al. Boise is putting together an undercover school. If you are interested give me a call." I was enthralled to hear the news. It had been almost two years since the civil suit had seemed to collapse the department's interest in undercover pursuits. The supervisor of the unit had moved on, and the department's one full time undercover officer had put the uniform back on and left the covert world. Al's message sparked more attention than the rancher that needed help with an elk depredation.

Although it was after dinner, there was no way I would wait until office hours the next day. Wardens don't work normal hours, and Al never seemed to mind getting called at home by one of his troops. Al informed me that the department had moved Special Investigations under assistant chief Roger Jones' umbrella and Roger had hired some "new guy" to fill the vacant undercover position. Between Roger and the new guy, they had scheduled a week-long undercover training session limited to two officers per region.

"I thought you'd be interested," Al said. "I'll throw in a good word in for you."

The conversation buoyed my spirits and I asked Al what he knew about the new guy.

"He's somebody Roger hired from the Secret Service and it sounds like he's keeping the guy's name quiet."

Some weeks later I drove to the training that was being given at the old ranch headquarters in Harriman State Park. We were told to drive private vehicles and no uniforms or have any other "cop stuff" showing. I have no idea what the department told the park personnel about the training, but I'm certain the "undercover" word wasn't mentioned.

At the training, there were a dozen other Idaho game wardens whom I knew well and were happy to see. All of them were spark plugs. Roger Jones, the head of SIU was there and two other faces that I didn't recognize. The first face belonged to Gary Burke, Montana Fish Wildlife, and Parks' undercover officer. Gary had a long career as a uniform Montana game warden before taking Montana's "special investigator" or undercover position. He had a reputation for cuddling up to wildlife crooks, gaining their confidence and then putting them in jail. Burke's cases were so successful that the Montana director had heavily bragged him up to Idaho's director Jerry Conely. Conley must have been listening since he reinvigorated the department's undercover program. Idaho's "new program" was standing next to Burke. He was introduced as Mike Best. His 250 pound, 6'4" frame made him the biggest person in the room. Idaho had historically filled its undercover position from within its uniform ranks. So who was this Mike guy? Did he know what he was doing?

Roger's introduction included Mike's history as an agent for the Secret Service. He'd worked numerous undercover cases involving counterfeiting and credit card fraud, and had run a "storefront" where crooks could launder stolen Social Security checks–or rather they thought they could. The question the rest of us had was what does this new guy with the eastern accent know about catching wildlife crooks?

During the week, it became clear that Best had been recently working wildlife cases with Burke in Montana. Burke and Best started talking about cases they had been working together. I think it put most of us at ease to know that Burke was teaching our new guy the ropes about wildlife criminals.

But we were still concerned. Every game warden knows there are some cases you just can't *make* in uniform and we all knew we needed somebody to work those cases and potentially to assist in working covert cases.

The first evening after class I sat down with Mike overlooking the Henry's Fork River that twisted through the park. I knew the view well. When I was a kid, the property was owned by railroad magnate Averell Harriman and was rightly called the Railroad Ranch. Somehow my father had become friends with Harriman's manager, Ben Meese. Ben had given my dad a key to the ranch and told him that he and his family were welcome on the ranch anytime to fish, hunt, or just have dinner with he and his wife, Dean. The ranch consisted of 16,000 acres of wild country thick with moose, elk, bear and waterfowl. To top it off, Henry's Fork was full of large cutthroat and rainbows. Ben didn't allow hunting on the west side of the ranch since it was a primary wintering area for trumpeter swans but had no problem with us hunting ducks and geese on the east side. Dad had dug a pit blind next to the river, and we spent many a cold day hunting waterfowl from that pit. Harriman later willed the ranch to the State of Idaho, and it became one of the people's true wild gems as its first state park.

Mike and I talked about the view while sipping beer. I explained my family's connection with the ranch and reflected on a particular fall day in the duck pit with my brother Nick. Our parents had been with us in the morning for the early duck activity and had left us, at our request, to get in some midday shooting before their return in evening. Better to sit and watch for ducks than cut firewood with a bucksaw. Nick and I stayed in the pit and pass-shot ducks that kept flying by our decoys. When I say pass-shot, what I really mean is that we shot and shot, and never touched a bird. When our parents returned, the ground around the pit was littered with dozens of empty shotgun shells and no ducks.

Dad just looked at us, lifted his eyebrows a bit and said, "It looks like the ducks had a good afternoon."

Mike was friendly, articulate, and full of enthusiasm. His face never lost its smile. He eyes twinkled when he talked about his wife and three daughters. He almost bubbled when he talked about going after wildlife crooks. When I asked him about his limp he explained that he had injured his back during a Secret Service training exercise. They had been training new agents in motorcade procedures for executive protection. The lead vehicle was being driven by a recruit and had come around a corner to find a barricade of 55-gallon drums. Mike explained that the proper response was to accelerate through a blockage and assume it was part of an ambush. Unfortunately the rookie initially gunned the vehicle and then slammed on the brakes causing Mike's trailing vehicle to slam into the rookie's car. Mike explained the injury had caused enough nerve damage that his calf muscle had atrophied, and occasionally he needed a leg-brace.

I took this open door to explore his career with the Secret Service. It turned out that Mike had worked protection for Presidents Ford, Carter, and Reagan. And then he began talking about chasing counterfeiters.

"The worst thing you can do with a counterfeiter is to incarcerate him with a bunch of other counterfeiters," he explained. "They sit in there and talk for years about what paper and inks worked or didn't work, how they got caught, and they come out of prison with a PhD in counterfeiting."

I felt good about Mike. He was friendly, sensible, and had a keen love of wildlife. It was obvious he had gained a good foundation for working undercover wildlife cases with Burke. In watching the two interact with each other, it became obvious that Gary respected him.

Much of the class was spent on developing covers. A cover includes your fictitious name, residence, family, historical background, and occupation. You have to know your cover occupation, not just what it is, but know it to the point you can discuss the job at great length if need be. If you claim to be a stockbroker, you'd better know the Stock Market and have a good inside knowledge of how it functions. And also know how to avoid giving out financial advice that could haunt the case. Your cover has to give you a reason to be in the area and an excuse to return. You also have to know the city you are supposedly from and your state's politics and issues well enough to talk about them. Another problem with cover selection is choosing something that cannot be easily checked up on. If you claim to run a lumber yard, a series of phone calls by your target to your cover town will either "hink up" your target and shut the case down or seriously put your life at risk.

Burke talked about what he called the hink factor. He explained that "hinky" in the undercover world means your target is paranoid about undercovers.

"Some of them are so hinked up they believe everybody and their brother are cops. You'd think it would just be the druggies, but it's been my experience that most players have this fear," Burke said. "Once in a while you're going work a guy that has been poaching for so long without getting caught he's quit worrying about it. If your target is hinked up," he paused. "You *have* to know your cover backwards and forwards—he's going to drill you on it. It'll be the most important test you ever take."

Another major area the class covered was the issue of entrapment. Undercover work can be a constant dance with this issue. An example of entrapment is where a narcotics officer identifies someone who simply looks like a drug user; the officer has no knowledge of the character selling drugs, approaches him and offers them a $100 bill for some marijuana. Unless the target says something like, "I sell it by the ounce, and I sell a lot of it," it's entrapment. An officer has to be able to prove the target is "predisposed" to sell the contraband to make the case. If you get a tip about someone engaged in criminal activity, it's not predisposition; you have to corroborate it first. If the target has been convicted of the offense you are investigating, you're okay to open the door. Otherwise, you have to allow your target to make the offer first. You also have to consider what a jury will think about your behavior. In the marijuana example, if the target has been convicted three times for selling marijuana, you may legally solicit from him and avoid an entrapment defense. If the case goes to trial, however, the jury will never hear of the other convictions because of the "past bad acts" rule of evidence. You have to let the predisposition, or the criminal intent, roll out of your target as the case unfolds. Predisposition may take months to develop, and thus an undercover investigation can last a long time. Some have been known to take years. But, if you've got a valid crook, sooner or later, he'll dig a hole. Sometimes you just need to provide the shovel.

There were numerous other issues that were presented in the class. Burke and Best did a great job of reinforcing potential issues with actual case examples. Burke brought up a case he worked where the person was killing moose illegally and selling the meat.

"I worked a guy named Dakota. He was filthy, he gave me body lice twice," Burke paused and smiled. "Explain that to your wife when you come home after working a case and have lice crawling all over you."

After Burke had known Dakota for several months, Burke told him a story about a person causing him trouble. The guy in Burke's story was a fictitious part of his cover, and Dakota responded by offering to kill the troublemaker for $3,000. Burke discussed the turn of events with his prosecutor and they went after Dakota for the murder for hire using the fictitious character as bait after the money was paid. The case reinforced just how dangerous some wildlife criminals are and the fact that wildlife crooks are frequently involved in all sorts of criminal enterprises.

One point Burke made clear; "There is no back up waiting around the corner in some high tech van. If you get burned, it's up to you to figure out how to survive."

As Burke put it, "When you're under, you're on your own."

At the end of the class, Best and Burke went back to their clandestine world and I headed home ready for another fall of what some of us called the crazy season—hunting season. That fall was one of the craziest I ever had. I remember getting home one November night, and wondering what direction the blinking light on my machine was going to send me off to. I sat down with the phone log and began taking notes as the machine beeped. When I was done listening and writing I had twenty-six hot calls to address. Illegal elk, deer, and a calf moose were on the list and it was already 8 p.m. I put the moose case at the top of the list and got busy returning phone calls. I didn't solve the moose case and it still pisses me off.

After things settled down a bit in December, I had a message on the machine from Mike Best wanting me to call him. I immediately called his home, and he asked whether I would be able to work an undercover case with him in Orofino. Mike specifically wanted to know whether my face was known around the Clearwater country and if I would feel comfortable working with him. Since I really hadn't been in the Orofino area for twenty years, I didn't think it would be a problem; the only people who really knew me there were the game wardens. Surely working with Mike wouldn't be an issue. I'd had a good feeling about Mike while having that beer with him on the Henry's Fork and was eager to get to work.

Mike explained that Bill Snow, the District Conservation Officer in Orofino, had developed information that a Nez Perce tribal member was selling wild game meat through a bed and breakfast called the Crabtree in nearby Ahsahka and the place was owned by a non-tribal member.

I told Mike I was eager to work it but would have to clear the request through my new boss. Mike explained that he would book a weeklong reservation at the bed and breakfast in January for us, and we would go in posing as steelhead fishermen.

We talked about suitable covers. I had worked as a wild-land firefighter for fifteen years, mostly in Alaska, and worked with numerous smokejumpers. I had candidly wanted to be a jumper but had never gotten the opportunity. My brother and his family were living in Hailey, and I was sure they could check an undercover mailbox for me from time to time. Now for a name. My grandparent's name was Henderson. Thus, smokejumper Tony Henderson from Hailey, Idaho was born. Mike said it sounded okay to him and he'd facilitate my undercover driver's license, and I'd have to make arrange for an undercover telephone line. Mike gave me the contact with the telephone company and explained that the phone number would have a Hailey prefix but would be set up on a call forwarding into my home landline. It would be time to change the message on my machine. No more, "Hello, you've reached the game warden." It was soon to say, "Hello, this is Tony, please leave your name and number."

I wasn't surprised by the information Snow wanted us to investigate. The first time I heard about Nez Perce tribal members selling wild game meat was from a professor at the University of Idaho who complained about it during a P.E. class. I had also heard grumblings from other wardens around the state about the problem of tribal members selling wildlife in the Clearwater country.

Before I hung up, Mike's voice dropped in pitch and he said, "Only Snow, my boss Roger, you, and me are in the loop on this. Don't tell a soul about where we are headed or what we are up to."

The next morning it was time to bounce it off my new boss and I was a bit antsy about it. I'd decided I'd grow a beard for the assignment so I hadn't shaved that morning, and despite putting on a clean uniform I looked a bit rough. I drove the twenty-one miles to Salmon wondering what Ed's response was going to be. Al Nicholson had moved up the ladder, and I had a new supervisor who was an enigma. The visit would be a courtesy since there were few legitimate reasons for a first level supervisor to turn down a request from headquarters—but I was still nervous about it. Ed was sitting at his desk processing paperwork. I informed him that I had been asked by Roger Jones of SIU to work an undercover case with Mike Best. He asked me who Best was, and I explained he had been our undercover operative for the last year. I explained that it would take some prep work and we'd be gone for a week in January.

"I was wondering why you hadn't shaved this morning," Ed commented and paused. "What're you going to be working on?"

The pause in the conversation told me that he wasn't happy about what I had just said.

"You know," I answered. "I can't talk about it but it sounds like we've got good information."

"Well, I guess it's okay, I'll have to figure out who'll take your calls."

His attitude was clearly negative. Maybe Ed's posture was leftover residue from the last undercover case. Maybe it was the fact he'd never worked undercover.

I called Mike back and told him I had permission from my boss—I didn't candy coat it with the word "blessing." Mike said he'd called Bill Snow back and got a bit more information about the case. Snow had told him the proprietor of the Crabtree Bed and Breakfast was Rex Lubinski. There was little known about him other than he was from Wisconsin and was supposedly associated with the right wing Posse Comitatus extremist group. The local sheriff had obtained a Polaroid photograph of Lubinski in his lodge standing next to a pile of weapons, including what looked like machine guns.

I had heard of the extremist group but asked Mike what he knew about it. Mike explained that they believe there are no legitimate government above the county level and no higher law enforcement authority than the county sheriff. "They were involved in two shootouts in the Midwest, a couple of marshals and a sheriff were killed," Mike said.

He went on to expand on the information about the tribal member providing the meat. "The Indian is Jimmy Charbonneau. Snow says Charbonneau has been selling elk, moose, and steelhead for a long time. He attacked an FBI agent with a rock; I'm surprised he didn't get shot."

Great, I thought, *no undercover experience, and I was going to get my feet wet with these two? What was I getting into?*

Chapter 3

Into the Clearwater

The Clearwater is a remarkable Idaho river that flows into the Snake River at Lewiston. It's formed by large tributaries that include the Lochsa River, the Selway River, and its North and South Forks. They're all big rivers running through bigger country. The heavy precipitation that feeds these rivers grows trees that reflect the size of its rivers. In the upper reaches of the Clearwater there are cedar trees over 3,000 years old; some reach 11 feet in diameter. It's my experience that it rains or snows there all winter long, the sun comes out for two or three months in the summer, and then it starts raining and snowing again. The sub-canopy vegetation reflects the regions heavy precipitation that produces a jungle of thick brush and ferns similar to the rainforest of the Cascades.

Lewis and Clark's Corps of Discovery limped down the Clearwater in October of 1805. When they ran into the Nez Perce Indians, they were in a state of starvation. Any horses that hadn't died or been butchered for food were lame. The Corps was about done for, and history balanced like a teeter-totter. The Nez Perce rose to the occasion and chose to help with food and harbor horses while the Corps pressed on to the Pacific with freshly made dugout canoes.

Today, I'm quite sure one wouldn't have to spend much time finding a Nez Perce who questions their forefathers decision to help the explorers. One Nez Perce I met on this investigation referred to me (a fourth generation Idahoan) as a European and I'm certain he believes it was a *big* mistake.

Forty miles upriver from the Clearwater's confluence with the Snake is the town of Orofino. From census to census, it bounces around 3,000 folks. On the north side of the town a lumber mill is fed by loggers who justifiably believe they are an endangered species. On the west side of town, the State of Idaho has a 55 bed psychiatric facility that inspired the high school motto: "Home of The Maniacs." Orofino is the Clearwater County seat and accordingly the location of the courthouse and prosecutor's office. There is also a state prison on the west side of town. Sheriff Nick Albers told me that when a prisoner is incarcerated at the facility, his family frequently follows. When the inmate is released they stay put. This may be one reason why there are more convicted felons per capita in Clearwater County than any other county in Idaho.

Four miles below Orofino lays Ahsahka and the confluence of the North Fork of the Clearwater. As near as I can tell, Ahsahka is a bastardization of the Nez Perce language referring to the North Fork's confluence with the main Clearwater. Ahsahka was a long established winter camp for the tribe. Anthropologists believe Indians used Ahsahka for at least 10,000 years. The Nez Perce believe they have lived there since time immemorial and I believe the Indians come closer to the mark.

The Clearwater crawls with whitetail deer. Elk are highly visible in the winter and moose are not uncommon. Steelhead and Chinook salmon run up all its tributaries except the North Fork, which is plugged by the dam.

Historically the Nez Perce lived a subsistence lifestyle, migrating from one resource to the next, dictated by the seasonal movements of the wildlife. Today, they attempt to maintain at least a part of that culture as best they can and I'm sure it's the reason the tribe keeps the hunting season open year 'round.

A federally funded fish hatchery dominates the Ahsahka community. The U.S. Fish and Wildlife Service and the Nez Perce tribe jointly manage it. The hatchery was constructed in an attempt to mitigate the elimination of wild salmon and steelhead runs that the dam wiped out. Depending on the season, salmon and steelhead stack up at the mouth of the hatchery and you can watch tribal members snagging fish there using heavy fishing poles and weighted treble hooks.

*****

I'd been on and off the phone with Mike discussing details of our pending trip to Orofino. He'd helped me with my cover by asking questions about "Tony Henderson." In return I ask him for details of his cover so I could learn about this character whom I had supposedly known for years. His cover was a traveling salesman for medical equipment based out of California. I supposed his only worry was the possibility of running into a doctor or nurse that would start asking questions. When I bounced questions back at Mike, however, he had an uncanny ability to think on his feet. I really didn't believe I was in his league and was anxious about our pending trip. Looking back on Mike's smoothness I'm certain he'd used the same cover with Burke in Montana and probably with the Secret Service. The name he was using was Peyton Parker. I'd never heard of the name Peyton beforehand and told him I'd call him "Pate" for short.

Mike explained, "He was my favorite uncle, I chose his name out of respect."

I found it curious that we were both using the names of relatives we admired. I surely felt that I was honoring the Henderson name and Mike was doing the same thing.

Our plan was to take his undercover truck with our fishing tackle and tow a department owned drift boat so we could look and act like steelheaders.

"Make damn sure that boat is clean," Mike instructed.

He wasn't talking about dirt. He was talking about junk from game wardens that might burn us. The boat had never had a department emblem on it. I'd gotten an undercover license plate for its trailer, threw in a couple of smashed beer cans, and I felt it was *clean*.

*****

The first "arrest" I made was as a sophomore in high school. My mother had bought me a fine warm down coat and had sewn my name into the lining. It wasn't cheap and I'm sure it set the family back. I'd had it about a week when it disappeared from my locker. I was dumbstruck. I'd never had anything stolen from me, and I was really proud of that coat. Mom and dad were upset when they heard about it and the their mood added to my dismay. About a week later I was standing at my locker talking to my friend Rex Ochi when my coat walked by. I'd seen him before; he had a fast car and smoked in the parking lot. The guy was a year older and a known "hood." I pointed the guy out to Rex and told him it was my coat and we were going to get it back. I'll never forget the look on Rex's face: Fear. His response might have been fed by the fact I was pissed and probably had smoke coming out of my ears. Here were my coat and the prick that had stolen it. Despite Rex's fear, he followed me over to the guy and I confronted him. He claimed innocence, but I grabbed my coat with him in it and said we were going to the principal's office. Oddly he didn't try to break away. I must have weighed 115 pounds and Rex was pushing 90. The red headed prick was probably 150. When we got to the principal's office, I told the secretary what was going on. That's when a bald guy wearing a sport coat and tie stuck his head out of the principal's door. I'll never forget what he said.

"I'm Detective Nelson with the Idaho Falls Police Department. I'm investigating coat thefts."

It was my lucky day. I showed him my name inside the lining and left with my coat. I'm still a bit amazed by the incident.

Mike reminded me that since we would be staying in Lubinski's bed and breakfast our gear would be vulnerable during the day when we were out fishing. He said Burke had told him it was common to have bad guys secretly go through your gear. Mike told me to make sure my clothes and gear were "clean." That meant anything with my real name on it was taboo. *Shit*, I thought, *everything I own has my name on it*. Ever since losing my coat I had habitually labeled my clothing, fishing, and hunting gear with my name. I had to scramble to find clothing and fishing gear that didn't have my name on it. This assignment started a 20-year streak of no more "Latham" marked on my clothing and equipment. I had a new cooler that had escaped my black marker; I labeled it with Tony Henderson of Hailey, Idaho.

I put together an undercover wallet. It had my Henderson driver's license and a few business cards that I had picked up here and there in Hailey when I had gotten my undercover post office box. None of them had any connection to the real Tony. It also had my undercover fishing and steelhead tag along with a hundred dollars of my own money. I had to memorize my new phone number and practiced a new signature. The whole cover issue was weird; I was learning a big lie.

I didn't want to go on this trip unarmed. My Glock 23 had Idaho Fish and Game engraved on the slide. It *screamed* warden. It would have been stupid to throw it in. I had a snub-nosed, five shot .38 stainless steel Smith and Wesson Model 60. I had bobbed the hammer so I could draw it from a coat pocket without hanging up. It didn't have near the firepower as my fourteen round Glock, but in a close-quarter fight for your life, it could deliver five rounds under four-seconds. Although the gun was compact, carrying it concealed was a challenge. Forget about ankle holsters. They make you walk funny, and they bulge your pant leg out–giving the weapon up. Sit down in a reclining chair and there's your gun. After looking my gear over I stuffed the loaded weapon and five extra rounds inside my daypack deep into its water-bladder pocket.

Most of the calls I had been getting on my answering machine were from the sheriff's office reporting road-cripples that needed to be euthanized. It was January, and the snow had pushed the elk and deer down next to the highway. Tomorrow I was heading out for the Crabtree so that night I turned my message machine off. I'd hitched the drift boat onto my truck's stinger. My gear was loaded in the cab and I was committed. It would have been bad to leave for a week and come home to twenty or thirty unreturned messages. Calls would have to go to another warden. I'd called my boss and reminded him I was leaving. He wished me good luck.

The part of this assignment that was grinding on me was my dog. Ben was a yellow half-lab, half-golden retriever who thought he was human. He was my daily companion on patrols whether they were by foot, vehicle, horse, or jet boat. He had helped locate dead critters on several investigations and his friendly personality frequently broke the ice with sportsmen. It was killing me that he was going to have to spend the week at the kennel. But next morning I dropped him off and began the five-hour drive from Salmon to McCall where I would meet Mike. The drive went across central Idaho through Stanley Basin, one of the most scenic places in the West. We'd agreed to meet at the fish hatchery. When I turned off the highway at McCall into the hatchery I realized I was following Mike's rig into the parking lot. We hitched the drift boat up to his undercover rig and I parked my marked truck, grabbed my gear and we headed north to the Clearwater with three hours to get "in role" and make sure we had our covers straight.

We crossed the Clearwater and gassed up in Orofino. I felt myself tensing up for the first contact. Mike must have sensed my trepidation; he turned to me and said, "Hey, relax, Henderson. You'll do just fine. Let's just go slow. We'll see what we can find out about this Lubinski guy."

The Crabtree Bed and Breakfast was west of Ahsahka, across the North Fork and up on a bench on the side of the timbered canyon. We turned into its driveway at dark. Showtime. It was a large two-story wood framed lodge with a double garage. Despite some junk here and there, it didn't look too bad.

Rex Lubinski looked more like a middle age biker than a businessman. He met us at the door with a grin that was missing a tooth. He was 5'8", a bit skinny, scraggly long hair and a beard to match. He was dressed in faded black jeans and a crumpled plaid shirt with the tail untucked. His wallet was chained to his belt.

He showed us into the combination dining and kitchen area and pointed to an open package of meat that was labeled "M-Steak" with a black felt marker on its butcher paper wrapping. Lubinski smiled and said, "I'll get dinner going in a minute."

The meat was dark and un-marbled. It looked too dark for elk meat and was much too lean for beef. *Looks like moose,* I thought. Mike asked Rex where to park and the two went out front. I took out my pocketknife and cut off a chunk of the mystery meat, stuck it loose in my fleece coat pocket, and quickly walked over to his sink to wash the blood off my hands.

Rex and Mike returned and Rex showed us our room on the second floor.

"Here you go," Rex explained. "Yous guys just make yourself at home, I'll get us some dinner going," he turned and I heard him walk down the stairs.

Mike whispered, "Careful what you say, it could be bugged."

I hadn't thought about the place being wired and his suggestion was quite sobering.

We went back downstairs and sat down at the dining room table and were introduced to a theme that was going to replay like a scratched record. Rex was drinking out of a blue can of Keystone beer. He pulled two cold ones out of the refrigerator and handed them to us. I popped the top and took a drink. *Gawd,* I thought, *this stuff tastes like bad water.* I liked good brown ale but this stuff was the exemplar of cheap beer.

This was the first time I had ever drunk alcohol on the job. Drinking in uniform is grounds for dismissal.

Drinking while working undercover is normal and covered by departmental policy. Getting smashed is taboo and could easily cause you to stumble on your cover. Burke had explained the alcohol problem. "When the stuff comes out it's a balancing act. You have to look like you're having a good time, but you have to figure out a way to remain sober." I was such a newbie at maintaining a cover I was half-assed scared to drink. But I was role-playing and couldn't screw it up. Time to drink and think.

We were posing as steelhead fishermen, so I asked Rex how the fishing had been.

"Jimmy's been catching a lot of them down at the hatchery," he said.

"What's he catching 'em on?"

"Hooks," Rex laughed. "Great big damned treble hooks baited with lead. Jimmy's an Indian; he snags 'em."

He had just confirmed part of our intel—his association with Jimmy Charbonneau. The meat he was about to cook us for dinner, for compensation, sure looked like game meat and if it were true, it would be the illegal sale of wild game. The bloody evidence was in my coat pocket. The information that Snow had developed looked to be true. We just needed to do some digging and prove what the meat was, how it was obtained, and that we'd paid for it. *And figure out whatever else was going on here.*

"Don't ask about this meat; tomorrow we'll have whitetail," Rex said giving us a sober glance.

I didn't ask, but his statement was important. It could be construed as an "inculpatory admission" in legalese. It indicated he had knowledge that whatever the meat turned out to be, it was illicit. I made a mental note of Rex's words to add to my future report.

Cleanliness was another matter. His hands were grimy and he didn't bother to wash them before cooking. Under the light of the kitchen area his clothing looked dirtier than it had under the porch light. *The glamour of undercover work,* I thought, *drinking cheap beer and eating dirty food.*

The conversation at dinner started off about the meal. Mike told Rex the meat was delicious and I backed up his claim. Rex said he went through a lot of meat at his bed and breakfast. I was thinking he was telling the truth. Rex switched the conversation and asked me what I did for a living. I told him about smokejumping. I'd heard plenty of jumper stories so it wasn't a challenge. I also explained that I was based out of Fairbanks and had to be back up there in April or May for training and would return to Hailey in September for hunting. The lying had begun.

I had to do something about the meat sample in my coat pocket. There was little doubt in my mind it was moose, based on its appearance and taste, but no court would have allowed me to testify to that. We needed the bloody sample to be forensically tested and it had to be fresh for the tests to work. Today was Monday, and we were booked through Friday. What to do with the evidence? I told Rex I needed to take care of some bait in the truck and borrowed a zip lock bag from him. I'm sure

Mike was wondering what the hell I was up to. I went out into the dark and placed the meat inside the bag and hid it under the seat. It was January and the Crabtree was at about 2700' elevation so it wasn't getting that cold. The meat would be fine for the moment, but down on the river the temperature was getting into the fifties during the day. It really needed to be put in a secure evidence freezer.

All this skulking around, seizing evidence behind a defendant's back (not to mention the lying and drinking) was the polar opposite from what I had been doing as a uniformed patrol officer. Taking the meat wasn't a Fourth Amendment search and seizure issue; we had been invited into Lubinski's place of business, the evidence was in plain sight, and we had reasonable suspicion that it was "fruit of a crime" and thus it was a legal seizure. More or less. But under state law, you need to give the defendant a receipt for anything seized. However, if I gave Rex a receipt now we were done and out the door. The action I had taken on this seizure was to help develop Lubinski's predisposition to traffic in wild game. It wasn't enough to call an end to the charade since we needed to know how he got the meat and who killed it, but it was a good start on the case. We needed this to further our investigation from a legal standing and we also needed to show progress to Roger Jones, the case lead back in Boise when we got *out*. If we eventually charged Lubinski with this count, we'd let the lawyers argue over the legal minutia of the seizure.

Rex stepped out the back door and I told Mike I'd gotten a sample of the meat. We quietly discussed our options how to get the evidence transferred over to an officer the following day. I'd been up for fifteen hours and had driven over four hundred miles. The fatiguing part wasn't so much the normal part of the day; it was the stress of my first undercover experience of skulking and lying while being "in role." Mike and I headed to bed anticipating tomorrow's developments.

The following morning Rex had a big pot of black coffee waiting for us. Mike and I drank coffee at the table and chatted with him while he fixed us a breakfast of bacon and eggs. He was dressed in the same plaid shirt and black pants from the night before. It didn't appear that he had showered and again, no hand washing prior to cooking. So much for James Bond and glamorous women I'd watched on TV.

I'm not what you would call a morning person, and here I was *in role* and not quite awake yet from a fitful night. I'd been wound up when I hit the bed and it took a long time for sleep to take over. I was at wits end to avoid calling Mike by his real name. For the time, he was Pate and I was Henderson the jumper. Thus, the stress was already starting to kick in without the caffeine. Mike seemed comfortable and smooth. He absolutely had the gift of gab and was keeping Rex talking.

Rex served us out of his cast iron skillet, and we made fishing plans while eating. Rex suggested we float from the dam down to the hatchery. Before we'd left on this trip, I'd checked with the fish biologists in Salmon, and they had told me the steelheading on the Clearwater had been slow. Slow fishing for steelhead usually equates to no fish, not even a bite. And it looked like rain. Since I lived on the Salmon River, steelhead fishing was something I could do anytime. Thus I wasn't chomping at the bit to fish–especially slow fishing in the rain. But this was a work trip, not a fun trip and we were posing as fishermen. It was time to get to work.

Lubinski followed us down to the boat ramp below the dam on the North Fork. We unloaded the boat into the river, tied it up, and drove our rig and boat trailer to the pull out above the hatchery with Rex following us. At the lower ramp, we got in Rex's Dodge, and he gave us a ride back to the boat. During the drive, he told us the meat last night had been moose. Bingo. Mike told him it was delicious and I reinforced the compliment. I'm not a big fan of moose meat but that's not what Rex wanted to hear.

I jumped in the oarsman's seat, and Rex drove off. Finally, we could talk but we had to keep our voices down. If there is one thing game wardens know, sound walks on water and there were other fisherman on the bank. Our main discussion was about what information we had gained. Lubinski was selling meals consisting of wild game. We were almost certain he was getting it illegally from his Indian friend, but it was only speculation. Then there was the evidence that I had put in the truck the night before. This morning I had recovered it and flipped it under the boat's bow to keep it cold. Mike reached under the deck to look at the evidence in the baggie. When he came up he had a green sticker in his hand that was embossed with *Idaho Fish and Game* and a serial number.

Mike looked at me and smiled. "Hey buddy, you missed this."

It was what the department called a property sticker. All major property items were supposed to have one of the damn things. Had Rex found the label before Mike, the result would be a cold shoulder, and my days as Sean Connery would have come to a screeching halt. Had the label been unknowingly discovered by one of our targets later in this case it could have been fatal. To say my failing bothered me was an understatement.

We fished for three hours to maintain our cover but what we really needed was to get the meat sample to someone in enforcement. I rowed down to the boat dock and we loaded the boat on the trailer. Mike dialed Bill Snow's number from a pay phone in the parking lot above the boat ramp. We were hoping we could meet with him at a safe location and turn the evidence over. I heard Snow's machine answer, "Hello, you have Bill Snow with the Idaho Department..." followed by a beep.

Mike told the machine, "Hey Bill, it's Best, we need to talk, I'll get a hold of you tomorrow." This was before the days of cell phones.

We headed the forty miles downriver to the Lewiston Fish and Game office. It was Tuesday, and surely there would be a game warden we could turn the evidence over to. If Lubinski questioned us about not seeing us on the North Fork we were going to tell him we'd heard people were catching fish at the Pink House hole, which was downriver on the Main Clearwater, and we'd moved down to try our luck.

When we got to the Fish and Game office, I asked to talk to somebody in enforcement. The receptionist told us that there were no officers in—which proved the old adage; *you can never find a game warden when you need one.* I asked whether there was a biologist available and Bill Atkinson stuck his head out of an adjoining office. I told him we needed to talk in private. Mike and I stepped in to his office and Bill closed the door behind us. I introduced myself as officer Tony Latham from the Salmon office and explained we were working a case and needed to sign some evidence over to him that he could turn over to Dave Cadwallader, the District Conservation Officer.

The biologist started to ask questions about the case.

"Look Bill," I explained. "I really can't talk about what we're working on, it's sensitive."

Bill replied, "I know the Indians are selling fish up river."

I didn't respond, obviously, we had just fed his curiosity walking in looking a bit rough and he'd figured out we were working undercover. I thanked him and left a note for him to pass on to Cadwallader. The note made it clear that the sample was evidence and that I would call him with further instructions.

Mike and I headed back to Orofino and stopped for lunch with the rain falling down outside. We were not interested in sitting in a cold wet boat all day holding a fishing pole. We talked about the potential for Bill Atkinson to run his mouth about the investigation. If he did he did. We *had* to get the evidence taken care of.

Although Cadwallader wasn't in the loop on the case I knew him well enough to know he'd keep it quiet.

After milking several cups of coffee we left the restaurant and turned up the Ahsahka Grade and began to morph back as Peyton Parker and Tony Henderson. Time to get back in role. Rex greeted us at the door and quizzed us about the fishing. Twenty-four hours into the case and I could finally tell the truth to him, "Nothing, not a bite."

Sitting down at the table Rex gave us each a can of Keystone. I popped the tab and took a swallow. More dirty water. At least I was getting paid to drink it. Rex opened up a package of lean meat that was a lighter color than the previous night's meat.

"This's whitetail from last fall," Rex said. "I got three of 'em you know, all of 'em was bucks. 'Got 'em the same day. I'm not sure which one this is."

His story sunk in and I thought about whitetail hunting; some hunters *rattle* bucks in by clacking two antlers together imitating a mock battle, some ambush from tree stands over deer trails. Others *still-hunt* by sneaking slowly through the woods. "How do you hunt 'em," I asked.

"I hunt from the back of a pickup truck," Rex boasted.

Prior to leaving for Orofino Mike had gotten a copy of Lubinski's hunting license purchases for the previous year. He had bouoght one deer tag and one elk tag, just like the law allowed. Rex had just claimed he had killed three, two over the limit, and he was feeding one of them to us for dinner for compensation—and it sounded as though he had taken them illegally with the use of a motorized vehicle.

We ate dinner consisting of venison, spuds, and salad from a plastic bag. I didn't bother to try to catch Rex washing his hands. It wasn't going to happen. After dinner Mike and I helped Rex clear the table and we sat back down with three more cans of Keystone.

"You know," Mike said to Rex with his Virginian accent. "I've always wanted to hunt sheep. But the odds of me drawing an Idaho sheep tag as a Californian are about zero."

"That's no problem," Rex replied, "I'll put in for sheep and yous guys can hunt on my tag. We'll go up Sheep Mountain. I've seen 'em up there, lots of times."

"Where's this Sheep Mountain?" I asked.

He walked over to the adjoining living room and pulled a Clearwater National Forest map from a bookshelf, laid it on the table, and pointed to Sheep Mountain above Dworshak Reservoir. I had done a backpack trip into the region in my college days and had seen several white mountain goats but no tan sheep. And it hadn't looked like sheep habitat either. I was suspicious that Rex Lubinski, the truck hunter, was confused about sheep and goats.

Rex shifted the conversation from hunting to prostitution. By this time, his words were rolling together from alcohol. He explained that he and Jimmy Charbonneau were planning on setting up prostitutes at his bed and breakfast. Rex slurred, "I'm gonna go up to Stateline by Post Falls, there's plenty of whores up there, they can stay here at the Crabtree and we can have gambling too, I'll sell the lodge to Jimmy for a buck, he's an Indian and untouchable."

Tony Henderson sat listening to Rex and smiled, nodded, and took another swallow of Keystone, but the real Tony inside was doing the world's largest *mental eye roll*. I'd drink Lubinski's skanky beer to make this case but frolicking with prostitutes wouldn't happen. To begin with, I wasn't into it and secondly any sex would flush this case down the toilet. But I was enjoying listening to his crooked talk about his criminal deeds and plans.

Rex said that most of the meat in his freezer belonged to Jimmy, and he was just keeping it for him. That's when Mike stepped out with his shtick: "My friend Donny down in Woodland puts on a wild game-feed every year, it's a pretty big deal, he charges a hundred dollars a plate. He serves deer, quail, pheasants, antelope, ducks, geese, and crabs from Alaska, he makes a lot of money off it."

Rex had unlocked the door with his tale of two illegal deer, and was openly selling us meals made from wild game. He'd laid his predisposition to traffic on the table. But Mike had bowled me over with his carefully crafted statement. It wasn't a solicitation to purchase wild game; it was just a statement about a game-feed. Rex could have easily just let it pass by. In a sense, Mike had just handed Rex a shovel. What would he do with it?

Rex replied, "I'll sell you elk and moose if you want."

Chapter 4

Digging a Hole

I awoke the next morning wondering where I was for a second. I focused over at Mike still asleep in his bed. And then it all came flooding back. What Rex had told us about selling meat to us, the prostitution, the moose meat meal, and the three deer he had killed in the last fall from the back of a pickup. I could hardly believe what we had stepped into. Where was this case going? Mike and I had not had a chance to discuss it, and we had not been able to talk in the bedroom. We still had to operate under the assumption that the walls had ears. When we had returned to the lodge Mike and I had checked our gear to see whether it had been tampered with, and both of us quietly concluded it had not been touched. It appeared that Rex Lubinski had a hink factor of zero.

It was Wednesday. We'd been in the area for two nights but it seemed as though we'd been there for a week. Mike and I went downstairs and met Rex drinking coffee in his kitchen. It was drizzling outside. A set of whitetail antlers attached to a skull plate with five points on once side and four on the other sat on the table. I grabbed a mug and heard Mike ask about the antlers.

"This is one of the smaller ones I got," Rex said.

"Where's the biggest one?" Mike queried.

"I sold it for three-hundred bucks to a taxidermist," Rex replied.

I wanted to get more information about his hunting from a pickup truck but I was afraid he'd hink up if I started asking too many questions. It was my experience as a game warden that the only way you were going to shoot whitetails from a truck was at night while running a spotlight, plus, hunting from a motorized vehicle was illegal on its face. Hinking him up now just wasn't going to get us the answers.

Mike asked what the week's stay was going to cost us.

"Thirty bucks a night per person," Rex replied, "I can't legally charge for the meals so if you just pay me a gratuity that'll cover the food."

I interpreted Rex's explanation to mean that if he sold meals he'd need to be licensed by the Health Department and it was clear why he didn't want health inspectors dropping by; game meat couldn't be sold. And as far as calling it a gratuity, it was still the sale of game meat.

Mike and I grabbed a cup of coffee to go and headed out for the truck. I told Rex we'd probably head down river and fish somewhere around the Pink House hole. When we got in the truck, Mike suggested we try to get in touch with Bill Snow and meet him somewhere where he wasn't known. We headed for the pay phone at the boat ramp. Snow answered on the first ring. He agreed to meet us in an hour at a restaurant near Lewiston called Rusty's.

We drove on down the Clearwater and just short of Lewiston found the cafe. Mike parked behind an 18-

wheeler. Snow was already inside. Even wearing civvies, he looked like a cop. He was a middle-aged, in-shape, crew-cut guy who had been a Marine. He'd fought in the Huk campaign in the Philippines about the time I was in first grade. He was the poster boy for once a Marine, always a Marine. I'd met him my rookie year. I'd found his sense of humor as dry as sand and it'd taken me a week to figure it out. I later got to know all "his guys," the wardens he supervised in his district. It was clear they'd all go to the mat for him. He was a warden's warden and they liked working for him.

There were few people in the cafe. Bill assured us that he was not well known this far down the river and shouldn't be recognized. Bill sat facing the door just like any cop would. "If I see, anybody drive up who might know me I'll just get up and walk out," he said with a lowered voice. Bill told us how glad he was to see that his reports he had been sending in to Roger in Boise had finally gotten some attention. "I'd almost given up on him sending somebody in on this," he quietly exclaimed, "I've had multiple sources telling me about Lubinski, they all say he's selling meat, that he's getting from it Charbonneau and maybe some other Indians. Without you guys up here, there's no way that my crew and I are going to catch him selling."

We told Bill about the meat that Lubinski had been feeding us and told him about dropping the sample off with Bill Atkinson.

"I hope he keeps his mouth shut," he replied.

Mike and I made eye contact without speaking.

"Are there bighorns around Sheep Mountain above the reservoir?" I asked.

"No," Bill looked at me curiously. "We've got a good goat population up there but no sheep."

I explained why I had asked and Bill smiled and shook his head.

We told Bill about Rex's offer to sell us meat and Bill's face lit up like a yard light at dusk. I told Bill about the three deer and that we didn't sense any paranoia from him.

"Well," Bill replied, "If you get into Charbonneau, and I hope the hell you do, it may be different. He's been worked undercover before. He was taken down for selling fish."

Bill's statement jabbed me with a sharp stick. There was no possibility that Jimmy Charbonneau wasn't going to be suspicious of us. I wondered if the federal agent who had told me about his jerky-stand shtick hadn't been the undercover that had worked him. It almost had to be. I was so struck by this news that I didn't even think to ask for the details.

It was a one-cup meeting. Short and to the point. We'd briefed Bill and he'd shared some valuable knowledge with us. It was time for us to exit and get away from the known warden. He took off in his personal truck and Mike and I headed back up the Clearwater.

Now what to do? We had all day to kill. Time to reinforce our cover. We fished from the bank at the Pink House hole, ate lunch, fished, drank some coffee and fished some more. Nobody we talked to had caught a fish. Boredom.

Towards evening we headed up the Ahsahka Grade to Rex's lodge. This time I wasn't so stressed out. I knew I could play the Henderson role with Lubinski, but Snow's comment about Charbonneau's history and potential paranoia had me worried.

We walked into the Crabtree past Rex's hot tub. It didn't smell like a normal hot tub. I guessed it didn't have any chemicals in it. Rex was in the kitchen drinking a Keystone and either his accent had gotten thicker or he'd had a few other cans of beer. There was a package of meat on the counter. "M-Steak" was written on the white paper with a black marker. It looked exactly like the writing from the first night.

"It's from a two-year-old bull moose I shot with Jimmy," he explained.

In Idaho, drawing an antlered moose tag is a once in a lifetime lottery drawing. One bull moose in Idaho and you're done. Lubinski had no license history showing he'd ever had a moose tag. Not the strongest case in the world but another violation to start working on. We needed to shore up the case. Rex went on to say that he had used two moose, one elk, and five deer in the last year. *Not bad for a bed and breakfast operator that apparently lived alone,* I thought.

"You have any family?" Mike asked.

"Yeah," Rex answered. "I got a wife back in Wisconsin and two sons, they're twenty-four and twenty-seven. They're coming next week to hunt with Jimmy. They'll do the shooting and as long as Jimmy's along it's kinda okay."

Good gawd, I thought. It was January, the elk season had been closed for months and he'd arranged for his two boys to come to Idaho on a big game crime spree. It made me wonder if it was his father who had taught him how to break the law and he was passing it along into his gene pool or if he'd invented it himself.

We ate the moose with hash browns and Rex started to talk about lion hunting. "There are some local guys who would take you out just to help pay for their dog collars and gas," he offered.

Idaho highly regulates outfitters and guides. If the players that Rex had just mentioned were licensed, he would have probably referred to them as guides or outfitters and the cost of the hunt wouldn't be laundered as fuel and equipment. I was having a hard time keeping up with all of Rex's crimes and corrupted plans. Lubinski was a *crook,* it seemed like crime was the only thing he'd talk about.

After dinner Rex asked us whether we wanted to look for elk with a spotlight in the nearby fields. "Yous guys can't bring guns," he explained. "The game department has a *dee-pred-a-dation* hunt going and the wardens are probably up there, ya know."

As a warden, I frequently used the term *depredation* when dealing with big game animals feeding on agricultural crops. His gross mispronunciation of the word was so bad I had to think for a bit before I asked, "What's a dee-pred-a-dation hunt?"

"It's where the game department has special hunts to help out the farmers," Rex explained. "The hunts during the day and I wouldn't be surprised to see the wardens are up there watching the fields tonight. That's why we'd better not take a rifle."

We agreed to go spotlighting. The three of us walked out the front door following Rex towards his Dodge. I was wondering about Rex's blood alcohol level and how nuts it was going to be to let him drive. "Hey," Mike exclaimed, "No sense burning up your gas, man, let's take my rig, grab your spotlight."

Above the Crabtree, the canyon benched out a bit. There were farm fields cut by timbered draws that lead down to the river. The only animals we found in the fields were whitetails and if any were bucks they had long since shed their antlers.

I was getting into this undercover role. "You got a place to gut and hang a deer?" I asked.

He replied, "That's not a problem, the magpies and dogs'll clean up the mess, ya know."

We didn't have a rifle, and I didn't want to kill a deer. I just wanted to send a message about Tony Henderson.

Mike told Rex that we were going to fish hard the next day and asked him where he thought would be best. He suggested we float from the dam down to the hatchery again.

We awoke to a drizzle of rain the next morning. The fog kept drifting in and out from the Crabtree. It was going to be a soggy day. Rex fed us breakfast with a pot of coffee. Mike and I climbed into our rig, and Rex followed us down to the launch and helped us shuttle our truck and trailer to the pull out. We fished and floated in the rain. At one point I realized there was another drift boat bearing down on us. It held game wardens in wet rain gear. Dave Cadwallader was in the boat with two of his cohorts. They had no idea who Mike was and played it right. They showed no recognition of me and asked to see our licenses. We chatted a bit about how slow the fishing was, they handed our licenses back with wet hands and then they were gone.

It was a long cold wet day. No fish and no bites, but it was good to get away from Lubinski. When we returned to the Crabtree, he was drinking another beer at the doorway. When I walked by the indoor hot tub I recognized its odor—it smelled just like a swamp. I was cold, but I surely wasn't going to crawl into the tub.

Rex fixed us another meal of lean red meat. It looked and tasted like venison. Mike said, "This is good whitetail. It's as good as the deer back where I grew up in Virginia."

Rex just nodded and said, "Ya, one of 'em from last fall."

After dinner Rex suggested we should go down to the Jet Club in Orofino for drinks. Mike took control again by offering to drive his rig.

The interior of the Jet Club smelled of cigarettes and day-old beer. It took me a few moments to get used to the darkness. I could hear several people in back playing eight ball. A drunk sat at the bar talking gibberish to the bartender who was washing a glass. The barkeep had a dead eye and it was hard to tell if he was looking at us or at the drunk talking to him. I guessed there were twenty people drinking in the place, most were Indians. The whites looked more hostile than the Indians. I didn't feel overly conspicuous until I realized I was the only person in the joint wearing a baseball cap with the bill facing forward. At least my beard had grown out. I was glad my back was to the wall.

I rested my arm on the table and realized it was sticky from dried beer. The cocktail waitress greeted us and asked what we wanted to drink. She made no attempt to wipe the table down and I didn't bother to ask. Mike and I ordered bottled Budweiser. I wasn't sure about Mike's decision but I knew I wasn't interested in drinking from a glass washed in this dive.

Rex ordered a rum and Coke and we started talking about how slow the fishing had been. Rex told us that steelheading usually picked up in February. "Pate" and I talked about it and agreed we'd be back next month. After one round Mike suggested we go look for elk with the light. I was happy to get out of the obnoxious place and it was a good excuse to quit milking my one beer.

We drove up the road towards Dent Landing and began shining the spotlight on some fields. Rex told a story about being up in the same area on Christmas. "Jimmy had killed a deer; we saw some elk but, we were so fuckin' high we thought we were hallucinating," he said laughing.

Great, I thought, *illegal wildlife, prostitution, and now drugs*. I would have to lean on my imagination to forecast how much crap we were going to step in with Lubinski. One thing I wasn't going to do was express any interest in dope. I think the reason he'd brought it up was to feel us out about drugs and he probably wanted to smoke a joint. It was a door I didn't want to open.

On the way back into town Rex had us swing by Jimmy Charbonneau's place. Jimmy lived in a tiny camp trailer parked in front of a row of government Indian housing. A wind ravaged plastic tarp covered the roof of the trailer. Its wheels sat on blocks and it looked like it has been there for years. An electrical cord ran from the nearest house to the trailer's side. As we stepped out of Mike's truck, dogs began to bark but nobody seemed interested even though it was nearly midnight. A light came on inside the tiny abode, the door opened and there he was. The 330-pound body of Jimmy Charbonneau plugged the doorway and was illuminated by our headlights. He was stout but fat with a large gut that hung over his belt. Somebody had once told me to never trust a man that wore both suspenders and a belt, and here he was. I really didn't believe in the saying but it had stuck in my craw and got me thinking. Black unkempt hair sat like a hat above his big jowled face.

"Whadda want?" His voice was low and bearish. I didn't know whether he was unhappy about the late visit or if something else was afoot.

"You been catching any steelhead Jimmy?" Rex asked, "These two guys ain't having any luck," Rex continued. "You been getting any?"

"I ain't been catching," Jimmy growled. "But I'm ready to go do something."

I wasn't sure what was going on here. Did Charbonneau mean he hadn't been fishing or hadn't caught any? I had a distinct impression that Lubinski had brought us to buy steelhead even though we hadn't asked him to do it. If this was an effort by Rex to broker a deal either Jimmy didn't have fish to sell or he was suspicious with the sudden arrival of two strangers asking about fish in the middle of the night. And there was the enigma of his last comment, "I'm ready to go do something." What did that mean? There were two clear things about the visit: First, Jimmy wasn't interested in company, which didn't matter since there wasn't room in his trailer for anybody else. Second, Jimmy Charbonneau was intimidating.

We drove off and Rex smiled and explained, "When he says he's ready to go do something, he's in the mood to go hunting."

We crossed the river and headed up the Ahsahka Grade. On a horseshoe bend, Lubinski said he had to pee and told Mike to pull over. Mike complied, and we all got out. There was a granite rock the size of a small Volkswagen on the uphill side of the road painted with, "FUCK BILL SNOW" in black paint. While Lubinski peed on the rock I asked him who Bill Snow was.

"He's the fuckin' game warden," Rex said laughing.

All three of us got a good belly laugh out of it but for different reasons.

The next morning I awoke with a thought: Finally we were leaving and heading home. I was tired and I missed my dog. We'd been putting in fifteen to sixteen-hour days. It had been a long week. The time we'd spent with Lubinski "in role" had been fatiguing. I was pleased with what we had accomplished. We had our predisposition on him and he wanted to "play" as the saying goes, plus he'd introduced us to Charbonneau.

At breakfast "Pate" asked Rex whether he could take a package of moose meat back to California for his friend Donny to try. Rex agreed and pulled a package of meat out of the freezer labeled "M-Loin" and handed it to "Peyton Parker." Mike had just pulled off a much cleaner seizure of meat than I had. No skulking into the dark of the night with evidence that a defense attorney could argue was stolen. It also kept in motion the game-feed ruse that Mike had come up with, and I was sure it buoyed Rex's spirits with the smell of money.

Mike gave Rex a check for the week that included what he had referred to as a "gratuity" for the meals. Rex was happy he'd met us, and we were happy too.

Rex went on to say, "If your friend down there is going to want some game meat from me, just tell him to buy a small amount from a game farm and keep the receipt so it'll cover what I sell him."

"I think he's already doing something like that," Mike replied.

"How much do you think he'd be willing to pay for elk and moose?" Rex inquired.

"Well," Mike answered. "Beef is about three dollars a pound; I would think that'd be about right for moose and elk."

"Sounds reasonable to me," Rex said. "I should have whores when you come back."

Rex's repeatedly bringing up prostitutes was an enigma. Mike and I hadn't talked about women or sex and yet for some reason Lubinski just kept bringing up prostitution and his desire to have them apparently available for us. *This is crazy,* I thought. You'd think somebody trying to run a bed and breakfast would be smart enough to run it as such and not try to run it as a combination B & B and whorehouse. But the thought that started spinning around in my head was this: *On the next trip I'm going to have to put up with skanky whores while drinking Keystone.*

Mike and I drove down the grade, passed the Bill Snow Rock and headed towards McCall. I was elated and at the same time I felt like a brick had been taken off my back. We had gotten much farther this week than trying to get Lubinski to be comfortable with us. We had gotten plenty of predisposition and Mike had come up with a ruse to start doing business. We stopped in Grangeville, found a pay phone and called Roger's office in Boise. I stood close to Mike listening to the one-way conversation. He told Roger we were "out" and filled him in with the dirty details. Roger listened but didn't ask any questions. I thought it a bit odd, usually you can figure out what a supervisor is thinking by the questions he asks.

Mike and I didn't talk much between Grangeville and McCall. We parted ways in McCall and I headed for the Salmon River country. It was a long drive home.

I picked Ben up at the kennel on the way through Salmon and broke policy by loading him in the front seat. We were both enthusiastic to be back together. By the time I got to my house above North Fork it was dark. Old vehicle tracks under fresh snow showed somebody had been in my driveway. As I walked through the door behind Ben I glanced over at my message machine out of habit. My first reaction was that the power was off since the green light wasn't blinking and then I remembered: I'd turned it off before I'd left. *I don't think that machine had been off for four years.*

Chapter 5

Back to the Uniform

I awoke in my bed thinking how good it was going to be able to speak the truth. No more lying, at least not until the next trip to the land of the Bill Snow Rock. Somehow Ben had managed to sneak up on the bed during the night and I didn't complain.

I took a long hot shower, feeling the relaxed atmosphere of being in my own home. As the water ran over me, I thought about what I had to do. I needed to get cranking on a report that detailed everything that had transpired over the last five days, I had gear that needed unpacking, a big load of wash, my time sheet was overdue to my boss, and the drift boat needed to be put away.

I started a pot of coffee and looked for anything resembling breakfast in the refrigerator; it was bare. If I wanted breakfast, and I did, I would have to drive the mile down to the North Fork Cafe. On the way out the door, I turned my message machine back on.

North Fork is twenty-one winding miles from the town of Salmon. It's named after the tributary that is really just a large creek. It's not a town, just a combination restaurant, gas station, and post office sitting at the junction of Highway 93 and the Salmon River Road that dead ends 46 miles downriver at the edge of the wilderness. A couple of hundred people pick up their mail in North Fork and gossip with any familiar faces they might run into. It's a first-name only community.

It's a great place to be a game warden. The people are pro-wildlife and the majority are glad the warden lives nearby. Most of them are hunters that look forward to hunting season but at the same time they don't look forward to the annual migration of "flatlanders" from the Snake River Plain that infiltrate the area in the fall to hunt and fish. A percentage of the flatlanders were my primary fall challenge.

I had worked my first three warden years eighty miles upriver at Challis. I couldn't drive down Challis's half-mile Main Street without waving at somebody I'd ticketed or arrested. They invariably waved back, but I wondered if it wasn't a Pavlov's-dog reaction from a few. It was a good place to learn the art of game wardening in a small community. I'd found that if I applied the law equally and treated violators fairly I could still (hopefully) sit down and drink coffee with them after the smoke had cleared. The ones that held a grudge weren't worth losing sleep over. But when the North Fork job came open, I jumped on it.

I loaded Ben into the front of my personal truck and drove down to the North Fork Cafe wearing my civvies; I was still tired from the trip and had a desire to remain anonymous. I sat down at a vacant table and heard a guy behind me ask, "How's the game wintering?"

I turned without recognizing him, "Well I think things are fine right now but it depends on how much snow we get. Let's keep our fingers crossed." *So much for an undercover breakfast*, I thought.

When I got home the green light was blinking on my machine. I hit the play button. "Tony, this is the sheriff's office, somebody hit a deer at mile marker 342 and they think it's still alive, call me if you get this."

I hated to see critters suffer and really disliked putting down broken deer or elk, but it was a common occurrence, especially during the winter, along the North Fork of the Salmon. Of all the recurring game warden tasks, it was the one that I hated.

I changed from my civvies and put on my uniform. The outfit consisted of green Levis, a gray uniform shirt with shoulder patches and badge, the gun belt with pouches for handcuffs and a set of extra magazines for the Glock. I'd heard game wardens call the uniform different names. Warden Terry Williams had called it his costume, using the term the superheroes in the comics called their uniforms. I'd always had to laugh at this since the irony of it was that when it came to wildlife, Terry really was a superhero.

I unhitched the drift boat and dropped the tailgate. Ben jumped in the back and crawled into his padded kennel. I opened the driver's door and sat down in a familiar setting. The blue "Kojak" light was attached to the dashboard by a big magnet that sat on a steel plate. It was possible to use the light on the dash but it was so bright it made the practice impractical during the day and impossible at night. Most of the time you'd open the door, slap it on top of the truck's roof, and close the door. It was much more noticeable up high flashing 360°. If you tried to "run code" with the light on the roof, it would come off at about 105 miles per hour. If you managed to get the truck going above the magic 105, the light would come off, tethered by its cord and start pounding the top of the truck. It sounding as if somebody were up there with a big hammer smacking the roof. The speed limit set by the light's magnet wasn't a bad thing since four-wheel drive pickups weren't designed as race cars.

Below the dash was the two-way radio. The mike was clipped to the front of a wooden box sitting in the middle of the bench seat. I had made the box to act as my mobile desk. I could store paperwork inside and write on the top. It looked much newer than the one I had first seen in the warden's truck years ago and was held in place by strips of Velcro that kept it from sliding on the fabric of the seat. Behind the bench seat in an open case lay my Ruger Mini-14 semi-automatic .223 rifle. I'd scrimped for months for the rifle and had thought it should have been issued as standard equipment. I'd used it several times to put down crippled animals and the few times I'd had the rifle out during high-risk arrests it had justified my outlay. Fellow warden Jon Heggen and I had talked about rifles and he had referred to the personal purchase of long-guns by wardens as "life insurance" and it made sense. He preferred his short-barreled Winchester 12 gauge pump.

I fired up the engine and selected the Lemhi County sheriff's frequency, lifted the mike and keyed it with my thumb. "Sheriff, seven-two-five is ten-eight on the deer call."

My transmission was followed by a pause and then: "Seven-two-five, ten-four and thanks."

I'd just told the dispatcher I was en route to handle their reported incident–they wouldn't need to try to find another warden. Up the highway, I found a skid mark and a chunk of plastic grill that revealed the site. I pulled over and stuck my blue light on the roof, turned it on, and clicked on the emergency flashers. I drew my Glock as I stepped out of the truck anticipating the eyes of the injured deer. The doe was lying just off the pavement in the snow, I was grateful to find that it was dead and had probably been that way shortly after impact. It wasn't unusual for a driver to hit a deer and make the call just to make sure the animal didn't suffer in case it was still alive. Most people in Idaho were like that. They appreciated and respected wildlife. Most of them anyway.

Roadkill is just what it is. In my rookie months I had tried to salvage several. A fresh roadkill might look edible but once you've eviscerated and skinned one, you realize it's not food, just a mass of broken organs and bruised muscle—not anything the health department would call edible. I told Ben to stay and dropped the tailgate; he was no stranger to dead stuff in the back of his domain. The only dead critter he shied away from were bears. Dead lions didn't seem to bother him and deer and elk were the norm. I winched the deer into the truck bed and drove about a mile to what I called my dead-deer depository which was an out of the way piece on state land. I backed in and dumped the carcass. If I'd left the deer beside the road it would have been a reminder to slow down but it could also result in eagles and ravens struck while bloated with meat. I turned towards home, pulled the mike off the box and said, "Sheriff, seven-two-five. I'm clear from the deer incident on highway ninety-three."

When I walked through my door I was happy to see the machine was not blinking; I needed to get going on my report. I sat down at my desk and started by creating an outline of the events in a time-line fashion, and then added in the events and who'd said what. I didn't end up with anything that looked like a finished document that day, but by the following afternoon it was roughed out. I called Mike and read it to him; his memory refreshed mine, and I included his comments. I set it aside to let sit for a couple of days as a draft knowing my brain would kick in with something I'd left out.

We'd already planned to book another trip back to the Crabtree in a month. We talked about dates and settled on Thursday, the 7th of February. Mike said he'd give "Lube," as Snow had nicknamed him, a call and would set it up. I left a message on my boss's phone to let him know another trip was on the calendar.

I called Boise and learned there were no Lubinskis with license histories that matched the ages of Rex's two sons. I called Snow and told him what Lubinski had told us about his two kids and their impending hunting trip.

"I'll pass it on to my guys. They'll just assume it's coming from a confidential source."

By the end of the week my report had grown to twenty pages. It was too thick for my stapler. I hole-punched the pages and snapped them in a binder. I'd heard other officers talk about major cases requiring a case binder, but this was a first for me.

Mike called the following week. He'd called Lubinski and booked another trip for us. He had gotten Lube to talk about killing the bull moose he had fed us, and he had reiterated that he wanted to sell meat to Donny for his game feed. And it was all tape recorded.

I quizzed Mike about his ruse he'd used about Donny's-game-feed to elicit Lubinski's offer to sell us meat.

"Donny's my brother in-law in Woodland," Mike explained, "If Lube is willing, I'll get him to ship meat down to Donny. I'll give California Fish and Game a call and make sure they've got an evidence cooler we can use."

Mike had also asked Lubinski about the taxidermist he'd sold his largest whitetail antlers to and Mike had come up with ruse #2. He'd told Rex that I'd used my girlfriend's deer tag on a buck I had killed and I wanted the antlers mounted on a plaque but that I'd lost her tag. Lubinski had told him I could use his tag. Mike told me he'd already located some antlers to take north with us and explained that we could use the excuse to see if his taxidermist was dirty.

When I'd gotten back from Orofino, I put together a to-do list for the case. You'd think you could just work undercover and go home, but it wasn't even close to being that simple. It took a full five days just to get the report to the point I was satisfied with it. Then there were the follow up leads; these included attempting to figure out the first names of Lubinski's sons and figuring out who the taxidermist was.

I had called headquarters and ordered a statewide list of taxidermist. I went through the list knowing two things: Lube's taxidermist was female, and she was operating somewhere in the Orofino area. I came up with one name, Lisa Gardiner. I gave Snow a call and told him about what I had come up with.

"You should have just called me up Tony," Bill laughed. "There really aren't too many female taxidermists in Idaho. She lives above Lube's lodge. I don't know much about her but we had a tip on her a while back about some illegal deer she may have taken in. She's probably worth looking into if you guys find the time."

I'd also talked to warden Dave Cadwallader in the Lewiston Fish and Game office about the meat sample we'd left with Atkinson. I explained to him that I was working a case for SIU and couldn't give him any details, and he understood. I got the evidence number he had assigned to the sample and asked him to ship it to the U.S. Fish and Wildlife forensic lab in Ashland, Oregon. I'd also shipped off to the lab the package of meat that Mike had gotten Lubinski to volunteer.

I called the lab at Ashland and explained I had biological evidence headed their way and needed to talk to the person who would do the analysis.

After a pause I heard a female voice, "Hi, I'm Tina, I'll be working on your evidence, what have you got?" I explained I had two samples headed her way and needed them tested for species and gave her the evidence numbers.

"We believe that they're from moose, but they could be whitetail," I explained.

"I'll run both through a gel-based diffusion process to determine the scientific family and if the samples show positive proteins for cervid, I'll test them down to species using the electrophoresis process."

The analyst sounded attractive, heck she sounded cute—so I attempted to sound as if I knew what she was talking about. In reality the information about diffusion and electrophoresis sounded like voodoo, however, I knew she was talking about the deer family when she mentioned the word cervid but that was about it. Confused or not that call was the closest thing I'd come to a date in months.

Mike and I talked about our fast approaching trip back to the Clearwater. "Let's try to cuddle up to Jimmy this trip," Mike chortled. "We'll let him get comfortable with us but he's probably not going to be as easy as Lube."

I had to laugh. I could hear Mike smiling when he'd spoken about cuddling with Jimmy. I think Mike knew the big Indian intimidated me and he was messing with my head for his own entertainment.

We also talked about the taxidermist, Lisa Gardiner. Mike's plan was to continue with his ruse that I had killed a buck and used my make-believe girlfriend's tag to cover it. And subsequently I'd lost her tag. He explained that it would give us a look at the taxidermist's

ethics also send the message to Lube that Tony
Henderson was a crook.

Idaho Fish and Game regulates taxidermists. By
state law, taxidermist have to keep a logbook
documenting all wildlife parts they take in. The log
includes the person who killed the animal, what the item
is, the tag number, and date of kill. Gardiner couldn't
legally accept the antlers without a tag number. And it
had to be my tag number, not my girlfriend's or Lube's.
If Gardiner were law-abiding, she'd turn us away and
we'd be done with her.

We talked about the one-year statute of limitations.
Idaho State Code allowed for a prosecution to commence
within a year of the crime. The moose that Lubinski had
bragged about killing with Jimmy would toll after a year
from the time he killed it. The concept really pissed me
off. When a year had run from the date the trigger was
pulled, a wildlife crook was home free. It was different
with the unlawful possession; as long as a person still
had some part of the animal we could charge them. But
the take or killing was a different matter and we didn't
know the date Lubinski had committed the violation. If
we were going to charge him with it, we'd have to
somehow figure out an approximate kill date.

Mike sensed my frustration and said, "Just more stuff
we need to get out of him. He's a jabber box and we'll
figure it out." Mike finished the call by explaining that
things were all set up with Donny and he was excited
about helping out. If we bought meat that needed to be
shipped, he'd be ready for it.

I had not been able to come up with the first names of Lubinski's kids by using Idaho license history, we'd have to figure out a way to get their names out of Rex and we'd need something to corroborate his story. Snow had called. They had somehow confirmed Lube's kids had been at the Crabtree but had not been able to catch them in the hills hunting.

The one call I'd been anticipating finally arrived. "Tony, this is Tina in Ashland. I think I've got good news; both samples you sent are moose."

It was music to my ears, and not just because it was from the gal with the warm voice; her forensic work had confirmed that Lubinski had sold us two meals of moose meat.

As warden Al Nicholson had once put it, "A rock in the box."

Chapter 6

Drinking with Charbonneau

I met Mike at the hatchery in McCall, and again we switched the drift boat from my patrol vehicle to his undercover rig. Gary Burke had warned us during UC training not to talk like game wardens or cops. "Don't use the word antlers," Gary explained. "Call them horns. You guys call 'em antlers, crooks don't. Refer to your truck as a rig and not a vehicle. Vehicle is a cop term."

Burke had brought up other cop-like behaviors you had to stay away from such as holding a flashlight like a club over your left shoulder, shooting a pistol with a two handed Weaver Stance or sitting in a cafe facing the door. The one I didn't like was his no seat belt rule; I'd never felt right without wearing one. "Crooks," Gary explained, "don't wear seat belts. Don't wear one unless your crook does."

I put my gear in the bed of Mike's rig under the camper shell, and we headed north to Orofino. We started talking about the case. He had called Lubinski and told him that Donny and his girlfriend really liked the moose meat and Donny was interested in buying more. Rex had responded favorably towards the contrived story and was eager to discuss business details when we returned to the Crabtree.

We were both wondering how the Clearwater County prosecutor would view the sale of big game meat as a meal for a few dollars. Food for money might not have a great amount of jury appeal, especially if Lubinski ended up in front of a jury with a couple of members that weren't keen on wildlife laws. Snow had warned us that John Swain, the county prosecutor, wasn't famous for going after wildlife violators, but his assistant, Lee Squires, had shown promise. Somehow we needed to expand the case from buying meals to buying wildlife in quantity—assuming that was what was really going on.

In order for an investigator to do a thorough job he has to get emotionally involved with it. He has to get at least a little pissed about it. It's easy for a game warden to become emotionally bonded to an animal that has been trashed by a violator; however, it is frequently difficult to get a prosecutor to show the same enthusiasm. The sooner we could get a prosecutor up to speed on the case and give him some ownership the odds would increase that we would see an aggressive prosecution. I was dubious about meeting with the prosecutor in a small town like Orofino and not being seen by the wrong person, but it was a hurdle we would have to clear.

Mike and I got back into role by making up a story about what Pate Parker and Tony Henderson had been up to for the last month. The two stories we cooked up were about Pate being on his medical sales route covering Salt Lake City and Boise. I, or I should say Henderson had a girlfriend back in Hailey that he had been spending time with. I was happy about the girlfriend story for two reasons: The first was to give us an illicit ruse with the taxidermist and secondly, and more importantly to me was that if the lodge had become a whorehouse, I'd be able to say something about my lady friend to ward off the witches.

Besides worrying about the prostitutes Rex was trying to recruit, my other concern was Jimmy Charbonneau. I had found it easy to lie to Lubinski about my cover and was confident I could continue to deal with him. But the thought of doing the same with a 330 pound Indian who had attacked an FBI agent and had previously been worked undercover troubled me.

We drove north and crossed the Clearwater at the Orofino Bridge and turned downstream driving past the hatchery in Ahsahka. Once across the North Fork we headed up the Ahsahka Grade into the black timber. The headlights lit up the Bill Snow Rock and we both laughed. We found the driveway going into the Crabtree and pulled into the circular driveway. A dirty Chrysler K-car looking like it was a candidate for a demolition derby contest was parked in front of the lodge. I hoped it didn't belong to a prostitute.

I reversed my ball cap a la the Jet Club, and Henderson and Parker walked up to the Crabtree's front door—once again it was showtime. Rex Lubinski greeted us enthusiastically with two Keystone beers. He had a cheap cowboy hat on his head, black jeans that looked familiar, and a different dirty shirt. He smiled, handed us the beers, and said, "Yous guys come on in. I wanna introduce you to my new manager, Robert Deacon."

Robert looked like a bigger and fatter Rex with a lit cigarette hanging out of his mouth. He was in his forties

and unshaven. I was happy that Lubinski hadn't
introduce him as his new pimp.

I asked Rex about how the fishing had been. "Ya
know, I heard they opened up a gate somewhere, they're
starting to come up and Jimmy's been doing good
snagging at the hatchery. I got one from him for dinner.
If'n yous guys wanna buy some steelhead I can set it up
with him."

"It depends on how we do fishing this week," I
replied. "But how much does he get for 'em?"

"Five bucks or ten for a big one."

"Sounds good Rex," I said smiling. "But I hope to
catch my own."

I didn't want to appear too enthusiastic about buying
fish; but we had come to traffic, not to fish. What struck
me about our return to Rex's world was that it had taken
him less than two minutes to start talking about crime
again.

Robert started cooking dinner while Mike and I sat
down with our beers at the dining room table. Rex began
talking about his two sons. "They were here a week and
got two elk and wounded a third. I trailed it for a while
and decided it would be okay."

Mike laughed, "Hey buddy, didn't you teach your
young'uns how to shoot?"

"They only had their Wisconsin deer guns; they need
some bigger elk rifles," Rex laughed. "If you guys want,
maybe I can arrange a hunt this week."

I assumed he was talking about going along with
Charbonneau in much the same manner as his two sons
had. Charbonneau's tribal status would, theoretically,

launder the dead animals, and we would do the shooting (both of which were illegal). Neither Mike nor I acted overly enthusiastic. We didn't want to do the killing; we wanted the bad guys to do it. A jury would frown on an undercover game warden killing an animal closed-season. We wanted the jury to frown on the bad guys not us.

Robert served the steelhead and said, "I cleaned forty salmon here at the lodge last summer."

"Did you catch 'em?" I asked.

"No, Jimmy did."

Forty Chinook salmon from the Clearwater were a lot of fish. The runs had been so poor, mostly because of the dams, that the wild strain of Chinook had been petitioned for listing as "threatened" under the Endangered Species Act. Sea-run Chinook weigh between ten and twenty-five pounds apiece; thus Robert was talking north of six hundred pounds of fresh salmon. The picture begged the question: What did Jimmy do with them?

The following morning Lubinski cooked up his standard breakfast of eggs, hash browns and toast, washed down with coffee. I told Rex we had the deer horns from the buck I had gotten with my girlfriend's tag and wanted to know how to find his taxidermist. He drew a map on a paper towel and told us her name was Lisa.

"Her husband's a mean bastard. A great big fuckin' logger," he said frowning rolling his eyes.

Mike smiled, "We'll just have to go see if the bastard is home. We'll run up there, drop the horns off and go catch us a steelhead," Mike continued. "Where do you think we should fish?"

"They was catching them from the bank just below the dam the other day. I'd just leave your boat here and fish from the bank."

Mike and I grabbed our coats from the room and went outside. We unhitched the boat and drove up the road trying to decipher Rex's paper towel. After some head scratching we found a white singlewide trailer on a hillside with a wooden framed building set below it. A hand painted sign showed us we were at *Gardiner Taxidermy*.

A worn but attractive Lisa Gardiner met us at the trailer door. She was tall and lanky with long brown hair that framed a smile. Not the normal taxidermist I'd been around that smelled as if they'd just gutted a mule. For a second I thought I caught her eyes smiling at me. But I surely wasn't going to welcome a female coming onto me during a covert case, especially one married to a big, mean bastard.

"I've got a set of horns from a deer I got last fall," I told her. "I'd like them mounted on a plaque."

"Let's take a look at 'em," she said.

We walked over to the truck, and I pulled them out and handed the antlers to her.

"Nice muley," she commented. "It'll be sixty bucks when you pick 'em up. Come on down to the shop," She said walking towards the outbuilding. "I'll need your name and tag number for my log."

"It's my girlfriend's tag and I can't find the damn thing."

"Just get me a tag number in the next few days."

"We're staying down at the Crabtree with Lubinski," I said. "Rex said he had a tag I could use."

"C'mon in," she said as she opened the door.

Mike and I followed her in. We were greeted by the smell of wet hides and tanning solution. I'd been in several taxidermist shops and this one wasn't unique. A whitetail shoulder mount was bolted to a steel stand with a barstool sitting next to it. Silver pushpins surrounded both of its glass eyes holding the cape in place while it dried. There were several finished deer mounts staring from the wall. Numerous antlers hung upside down from the rafters. Yellowish foam deer forms were piled beside a chest freezer.

She handed me a receipt book and asked for my name and number. I took a pen and wrote down "Tony Henderson." For a second I panicked and couldn't remember my undercover number, but after a brief hesitation I wrote it out. I wondered if she'd caught my stumble.

"You can pick it up in two or three months. I prefer cash. I don't do credit cards. If you want me to ship it I'll need another thirty bucks. If I don't see you by July I'll get rid of it, and don't forget that tag number," she said with a bit of a frown.

She'd turned into a crab. I had no idea why her demeanor had changed. Maybe it was the no-tag status of my antlers. Maybe she had become suspicious of my phone number hesitation.

The contact had caused me to realize the hink factor in undercover work was a two way street. The undercover is always on the alert for a sign of paranoia (hink) from the target. At the same time, undercover has the same paranoid feeling for the opposite reason. The target is looking for something in you that tells them you're the law, and you are watching for a change in behavior that puts up a red flag. Lubinski was so unsuspicious of us he was stupid—would Charbonneau sense something different and wake him up?

Mike and I drove down the grade past Snow's Rock, turned left and headed up along the North Fork to the dam. We talked about Lisa Gardiner. She'd knowingly taken the antlers from an illegal deer into her possession. It wasn't the biggest issue in the world of wildlife crime, but at the very least, it was good information for Snow. And it made us wonder what else was going on in her shop.

I brought up the near on my phone number to Mike and asked whether he thought she'd caught it. "I saw you hesitate. But even if she noticed, it doesn't mean squat. Don't worry about it. If she's suspicious, she'll either call you and tell you to come get your horns or she'll call up Snow and turn us in. And that ain't gonna happen; she wants your sixty bucks."

Mike paused for a moment and glanced over at me and smiled. "There are two weaknesses you need to take advantage while working these crooks, greed and ego. They're the two Achilles' tendons that they all have; some have a greater problem with their egos and others more of a hunger for the money. I think Lube has both, he smells money and he needs his ego stroked, so don't forget to feed his ego."

We pulled in at the base of the dam; Mike locked the truck after we pulled out our rods and tackle box. There were three other anglers fishing the hole. Mike and I walked down, baited up with some salmon roe and cast in. The other three anglers paid us no attention but were in easy earshot. It was time for Henderson and Parker to fish and forget the warden talk.

Mike and I were fishing below the dam's power facilities. The outlet of the dam was on the far side of the river creating a cascade that was much too fast and steep for the hatchery steelhead that still retained the urge to follow the trail of their wild ancestors. The dam was the end of the line for the steelhead and salmon runs. Its height precluded the building of a fish ladder, and the reservoir above the dam had buried the spawning and rearing habit for the fish.

I looked up at the top of Dworshak, towering 717 feet. I thought about the time my brother and I had driven up to this point to look at it. It had been a third as tall; the last log drive was running down the river and the last run of wild steelhead were running up to their doom. The collision of these two histories was nothing more than a memory—changed forever by a giant wall of aging concrete built in a harebrained effort to keep Portland, Oregon from flooding.

A loud splash interrupted my thoughts. One of the other anglers had just hooked a steelhead. Its yard-long body broke the surface a second time and then the man's line went slack. The angler cussed and the fish was gone.

That steelhead had been hatched in the Dworshak Hatchery four years ago, it'd spent a year in the rearing ponds and had been released into the river when it was four inches long to find its way down through four dams on the Snake and four on the Columbia (along with navigating the eight lake-like reservoirs above each dam). Its physiology had morphed from a fresh water fish into a saltwater resident when it found the Pacific. This sea-run rainbow lived as an ocean predator for three years growing to twenty pounds before following its ancient instincts to return to spawn in its natal waters at Ahsahka. As far as I was concerned, anybody who wasn't awestruck by this cycle was from a different planet.

I quit pretending I was fishing and started paying attention to my sinker dragging on the bottom, hoping to detect the slight pause or tap of a steelhead gently taking my bait. I think the sea-run fish we had seen must have done the same to Mike since our conversation had tapered off.

A green American Motors Gremlin drove up and parked beside Mike's truck. Recently the model had been included on the list of the worst-50 cars ever manufactured. Rex Lubinski stepped out of it, grabbed a fishing pole and a six-pack of Keystone and walked down to us. I told Rex about the fish and asked about the Gremlin.

"It's a '78; I just got it back from a friend I'd loaned it to. It's actually a good rig."

The two are a match made in heaven, I thought.

I told Rex to help himself to our bait. He was wearing his brown cowboy hat with the feather I'd noticed the night of the Jet Club. As he bent down to the bait, I got a close look at it and decided it was an eagle feather.

"So," I said. "Is that a chicken-hawk feather you got there?"

"It's an eagle feather Jimmy gave me," he bragged. "It's big medicine for an Indian to give you one."

Big medicine my-ass, I thought. It was illegal for Rex to possess it and it was illegal for Jimmy to give it to him. Indians were allowed under federal law to possess eagle feathers for ceremonial purposes and they could obtain them from the Federal Eagle Depository where seized and electrocuted eagles ended up. If we could seize the feather when this case went down it would be another charge against Lubinski.

We fished for three more hours with little conversation other than Rex bringing up the possibilities of a hunt later in the week. Neither Mike nor I asked for any details. Rex kept bringing up the illegal hunt about as frequently as he had been talking about prostitutes. I wondered if he would ever come through with either.

It was getting late, and Rex suggested we should head back up to the lodge for dinner. We walked up to the road, and I noticed he'd left his empty beer cans at the river. Rex took off ahead of us in his Gremlin, and I took the opportunity to run down and grab his trash, not sure if my effort were for evidence for a litter charge or if I were just disgusted with his slovenliness. As a patrol officer, my favorite quick-and-dirty ticket was a beer-can-out-the-window citation. I hated litterbugs.

On the grade back up to the lodge we passed Rex taking a pee on Snow's Rock. Mike honked and we both waved, Rex waved back with his left hand. Mike and I both laughed at the ludicrousness of the scene and the irony of Lubinski waving at two game wardens while peeing on the name of another.

The Crabtree was dark when we got there. Rex turned behind us and parked his Gremlin. He walked in with us. When we got to the hot tub he lifted the lid up and encouraged us to use it while he got dinner going. The tub's water was the color of Keystone beer. I grumbled something about having skin problems to Rex. Mike and I had already nicknamed it the 500-gallon Petri dish because of its smell.

There was a package of moose meat thawing on the counter. Rex pulled three Keystones out of the refrigerator, handed one to each of us and popped the third one. He'd drunk at least four while we were fishing. I walked over to the kitchen sink and washed my hands, hoping it would cause him to mimic my behavior before he started cooking. My effort was in vain, he used his salmon egg stained hands to prep the meal.

Dinner was uneventful other than another meal of moose. Rex's conversation oddly stayed away from talking about crimes or criminal proposals. I was curious of what had happened to his prostitution plan but had no intention of expressing interest in whores.

"I'm going to go get Jimmy," Rex said out of the blue.

His declaration was a head turner. The fact that he was bringing Jimmy Charbonneau up to the lodge surely got my attention. It had been a long day—we had met a dirty taxidermist who had stressed me a bit and I had discovered Lubinski's eagle feather but all in all it had been boring. With Charbonneau en route it was showtime.

Thirty minutes later Rex was back with Charbonneau and a skinny young Indian who looked as if he were about twenty. Jimmy's presence was overpowering, he was actually on the short side but almost as wide as he was tall. He looked powerful despite his gross gut hanging between his suspenders and over his belt. He was wearing blue jeans, a t-shirt and an unbuttoned plaid shirt. A black reversed ball cap topped his big head. Everything he wore was dirty and the odor of sweat seemed to hang on him. Big chunky fingers wrapped around a blue can of Keystone beer.

Jimmy eyeballed us as Rex performed a reasonable attempt at introductions. The younger Indian was named Newt. Rex didn't provide a last name and we weren't about to ask. The kid didn't say much and seemed as comfortable as a mouse in a mink farm. About the only thing that came out of his mouth was an occasional laugh in response to chatter that wasn't funny. He was nervous and just seemed to be tagging along with Charbonneau.

Jimmy was hard to read. He would make eye contact and then look away as he spoke with a low bear-like tone. He acted displaced but nothing like Newt. I felt friction in the air and assumed it was probably caused by the cultural polarity, but it left me wondering if it were something beyond the Indian/white issue.

Rex was a talker and Jimmy wasn't. He didn't seem all that interested in what Rex gabbed about, but he appeared to be listening to what we said. He was focused on us. *Is Jimmy hinked up or am I just being paranoid,* I wondered.

Rex and Mike kept the conversation going. I tried to add what I could. Jimmy mainly listened and Newt would sporadically laugh even though none of us were telling jokes. Charbonneau never cracked a smile. It was a bizarre event.

About an hour into the night, my impression was that what Jimmy and Rex had most in common were grunge and beer. Jimmy, however, won hands down in both the beer drinking and dirty contests. I'd lost track of how many beers Jimmy Charbonneau had downed, but it was at least six, maybe ten. I'd also noticed he had enough dirt under his fingernails to start a garden.

I had a sense that Charbonneau generally just tolerated Rex—their relationship might be more symbiotic than friendly, but my theory needed more time. Watching the two interact that evening precipitated the question: Why had Rex brought Jimmy up to the Crabtree? Had Jimmy come up for the beer or to check us out or both? Was Rex trying to broker a deal?

Chapter 7

Steelhead for Porn

Mike and I had headed for our beds with the three others still drinking in the living room. I would have loved to have left a tape recorder under the couch to listen to what they said about us. Maybe it was good, maybe it was bad, maybe Newt and Jimmy just sat drinking Rex's beer and listened to his banter.

When I awoke the next morning, I realized I hadn't heard the Gremlin leave in the night and didn't believe I'd slept that soundly. When we walked downstairs, the three were sitting around the dining table. Jimmy had a can of beer in his fist and Rex and Newt were drinking from coffee mugs. Numerous blue Keystone cans were lying about the living area from the night before along with the smell of flat beer.

Rex handed us mugs of coffee, and we sat down. As I took my first sip I wondered where Newt and Jimmy had slept. Rex had either given them a room or they had crashed on the two couches.

Jimmy seemed to have relaxed the tension he'd exhibited during the evening and Newt acted hung over. Curiously, Jimmy became talkative. "When I was arrested last summer for illegal salmon, the wardens missed five I had in a gunny sack." He smiled, exposing yellow teeth.

I didn't know how to respond to his statement. Mike and I were unaware of him getting in trouble over fish the previous summer. I couldn't even figure out how he could get in trouble with salmon unless it was on private property. I guessed he must have been talking about tribal wardens since it would explain why we hadn't known about it. The big question I was wondering was *why had he brought up a game warden story out of the blue?* Maybe he was fishing for a reaction from us; maybe he was just bragging.

"Well," Mike said. "You must be sneakier than the wardens."

"My fish sack was lying in the grass so I just walked over to the bastards and got away from it. They never even looked around for it," Jimmy sniggered.

Rex served up scrambled eggs and sausage links that had been warming in the oven.

"I traded a couple of steelhead last week for some marijuana," Jimmy added.

Mike replied, "You must be a better fisherman than we are 'cause we sure can't catch 'em!"

Mike had skirted the drug issue and focused on our cover with the fish talk. Simultaneously, he'd stroked Jimmy's ego by complimenting him on his cleverness in dealing with the wardens and his ability to catch fish.

Jimmy downplayed it, "I don't have to bait 'em like you white guys do, I just snag 'em down at the hatchery."

Mike used his gift of gab. He could sit at the table with this immense beer-drinking Indian and just talk. About all I could do was drink coffee, listen to Mike and Jimmy, and eat my breakfast. I noticed, however, that there was no plate in front of Jimmy. The rest of us were eating but Charbonneau was just drinking beer.

I turned to Jimmy. "Aren't you going to eat breakfast with us?"

"I don't eat no food when I'm drinking," he replied.

Jimmy raised his beer, finished it off and threw the empty can into the kitchen garbage like he was shooting hoops. He took his ball cap off and ran his sausage like fingers through his greasy hair.

"Well you got to eat, don't you?" Mike queried.

"I don't eat nothing when I'm on a toot."

I assumed he was talking about a binge. The night before Jimmy had drunk enough to get a horse smashed and his speech had never even become slurred. Either it was his size or his habituation or both. Either way I had never been around anybody that didn't eat food.

I stood up and picked up the coffee pot and brought it back to the table. "You want yours topped off Newt?" He nodded and I filled the four cups up, returned it to the counter and sat back down with my mug. It was the only communication I'd seen from Newt since we'd joined the crew that morning.

Mike turned to Jimmy, "Does the tribe do much at Christmas up here? Don't they have a big potlatch or something?"

"Not really," Jimmy answered. "Rex and I went driving around and hunting last Christmas. I was running the light and we seen a buck on my side," he glanced over at Rex and scowled. "He shot the fuckin' thing right out my window, right past my head."

Jimmy stood up and retrieved another beer from the fridge.

Rex smiled. "I got him with my .22 lever-action; that gun's killed a lot of deer."

Mike had just managed to get Charbonneau and Lubinski to talk about the Christmas buck. Rex had first told us that Jimmy had shot it, and now they both agreed that Rex had shot it. The confusion was probably explained by the dope they had been using that night. Either way, it was an illegal animal since the season was closed to Rex and Jimmy couldn't hunt with a non-tribal member.

"How big of buck was it?" Mike asked.

"I've still got the horns. Let me go find them," Rex stood up and headed to the garage. A moment later he came back in carrying a set of whitetail antlers connected by the skull plate. The antlers had two points on the right side with a distinctive small drop point below the main beam, and the left side had three points turning up from the beam. We had another rock in the box on Lubinski but would need to seize the antlers and the rifle at the raid phase of the case to help corroborate his statement.

Rex handed the rack to "Pate".

"That's not a bad buck," Mike said. "They still wearing their horns or have they dropped 'em?"

"I think they've all dropped," Jimmy answered. "I haven't seen a horn on one for a while."

Jimmy continued, "Rex says you're from California, eh?"

"Yeah," Mike answered. "Woodland, it's just west of Sacramento."

"I used to have a friend down in California," Jimmy said. "I gave him two or three elk and a moose, I think he must be dead now 'cause I haven't heard from him in a long, long time."

"Where in California?" Mike asked.

"I can't remember. 'Never been down there," Jimmy answered.

Mike and I finished our meal, and we told the trio we were headed back to the dam to fish. It was our cover and we had to maintain it. On the way down the hill, we talked about Charbonneau's last comment about his California friend. He'd used the word "gave" and not sold. It was a stretch to believe he had given away a half-ton of meat to a friend. But the fact that he had brought it up plus all the other talk about trading dope and fish gave us hope. Maybe he was beginning to trust us. Maybe it was the way he marketed his products.

We turned off the grade, followed the road up to the dam and parked. The guy who had lost the fish was back. I walked down with my rod and asked him whether he'd had any luck.

"I haven't had a bite."

We were back to steelhead fishing again. Mike and I went through the motions until about noon when Rex drove up in his Dodge and turned around and stopped. I could see Newt in the passenger seat. Rex rolled his window down. "We're headed to the Woodlot for burgers." We hollered up that we'd join them. The place was just a mile down the road, and we were bored, cold, and starving.

The Woodlot was a combination bar and restaurant with a pool table. As far as I could tell it was the only commercial endeavor in Ahsahka other than a couple of trailer lots. When I opened the door the warmth and the aroma of frying burgers hit me. Rex and Newt were sitting at a table drinking draft beer; other than the barkeep we had the place to ourselves. Mike and I ordered burgers and fries from the bartender and helped ourselves to a pot of hot coffee sitting at a nearby table.

"The steelies must be sleeping," I said. "I might have had a bite though."

"I caught three this morning at the hatchery but already got rid of 'em," Newt smiled.

"You must be using Jimmy's secret weapon," Mike said referring to Charbonneau's lead weighted treble hooks.

I hoped he would respond by telling us what he had done with the fish but he just gave us a grin and took a big bite out of his burger and chewed it open-mouthed.

About halfway through his chewing he turned to me, opened his mouth exposing his chewed-up burger and said, "I killed a big bull moose last winter and got $500 for the horns."

It was an admission that he was trafficking. The tribal code didn't allow the selling of any parts of game animals including the antlers. There were two problems with the statement. The first was that he had said it in such a boasting manner I doubted it was true, especially since $500 was a lot for moose antlers. The second problem with it was even if the story were true; the moose antlers were in the wind. They were gone.

Why he even brought it up was a bit of a riddle since the guy hardly ever spoke–but it probably had something to do with Mike's explanation of the greed and ego motivators. Another puzzle was why Lubinski, a middle aged white guy was hanging out with a twenty-year old Indian kid that had the personality of a sleeping house cat.

After we finished our burgers, Mike picked up the tab for Rex and Newt and told them we were going to head back to the dam and maybe catch a steelhead.

We got in Mike's rig and headed back up the road. "That kid will bring us some fish to buy," Mike said. I lowered my eyebrows and looked at him suspecting he was about to share a tidbit of wisdom. "Lubinski," Mike explained, "Is trying to hook the kid up to sell us fish. You watch. Rex will get something out of it too. But right now he's hustling me, you, and the kid."

We parked at the dam and started the casting ritual again. It was drizzling and cold. The man who had hooked yesterday's fish was gone. At least he had some brains.

The chill had set in after a while and I was tired of looking like a fisherman. I heard a rig coming up the road and saw Lubinski's Dodge headed our way. He pulled next to Mike's truck and I could see Newt in the passenger seat. I walked up carrying my rod and tackle box.

Rex walked around the rear of the truck. "Newt's got some steelhead," he declared matter-of-factly.

"Where they at?" I asked.

"One's right back here," Newt volunteered.

"Let me see what the damn things look like."

Rex opened up the truck's canopy hatch, and I stuck my head in. A 34", fourteen-pound steelhead was wedged between the tailgate and a chunk of firewood. It was a hook-jawed male with the classic rose-colored strip running along its side.

"What're you gonna do with it?" I asked staring at it.

"Sell it."

"To who?"

"I don't know yet," Newt responded.

"How much do you get?"

"Ten bucks a fish, I got six more too."

"Where they at?"

"Down by the Woodlot."

"How 'bout I give you fifteen for two of 'em?" I offered.

"Sure," Newt grinned.

I looked at him and smiled conspiratorially, "This is illegal isn't it?"

Newt hesitated, glanced away and replied, "Yeah."

"No problem," I said. "I'll just put them on my steelhead card for yesterday then."

"That's what everybody else does," Newt added.

Inside I was beaming. I had just pulled off my first illegal buy of wildlife. Sure, Mike and I had been buying wild game meals from Lubinski but this was the real deal. And it was a good case. I'd managed to get Newt to dig his hole and expound on the fact that he had an ongoing fish selling scheme going plus he'd acknowledged he knew it was illegal. And Lubinski was up to his eyeballs with aiding and abetting in the commission of a crime.

I walked over to Mike and told him that Newt had some fish for us, and I was going to buy two of them.

Rex told us to follow him down the road. Mike and I jumped in our rig and followed Lubinski down to a trailer lot next to the Woodlot. Mike pulled besides Rex's rig and I started to get out.

Newt heard my truck door, swiveled his head towards me and said, "Stay put."

I wasn't sure why he'd said it but I stayed in truck and watched. He disappeared behind a trailer for a few moments and reappeared carrying a heavy wet burlap sack. He walked to the tailgate of Lubinski's truck and dumped the contents. I got out and looked in the bed. Six additional steelhead, about fifty pounds of fish, were lying among Lubinski's firewood and beer cans.

"Good God Newt, that's a pile of fish," I said.

I pulled my wallet out and gave him a five and a ten for my two fish. Fifteen dollars for about twenty pounds of snagged hatchery steelhead. The buy was consummated.

Mike stuck his head in the truck and turned to Newt, "Hey, I'll take what you got left," Mike fished out two twenty-dollar bills and handed the money to the beaming kid.

Newt just took the cash with a big toothy grin and stuffed the green in his pants pocket without saying a word. Apparently, a fifty-five-dollar day was a big deal. Rex told us to leave the fish in his truck, and said he'd take them up to the lodge. He looked around nervously and turned back to me. "Don't bother putting them on your steelhead cards; it's okay for tribal members to give away fish."

We strolled into the Woodlot, and Mike bought four Budweiser bottles and passed them around. Rex took a couple of swallows and let out a small burp.

Mike put some quarters in the pool table and turned to Rex, "Lube, I'll bet we can whip these two in a game of eight ball."

We selected our cues. Mike racked the balls and invited Newt to take the break shot.

After a couple turns with the cues, Newt pulled a black butterfly knife out of his pocket and asked if I was interested in buying it. Mike had explained the greed motivator, and this was an opportunity to feed it. In reality, however, it was just my ego coming through. I wanted to be the first Idaho game warden to buy a butterfly knife in a bar while working undercover. I handed him a twenty and he gave me the knife along with another toothy smile.

After Mike and Rex whipped our butts in the game, we sat back down. Newt and Rex's beer were dry, and Mike ordered a second round for the two.

I turned to Rex, "We took those deer horns up to your taxidermist friend Lisa."

"She's a pretty foxy lady, eh?" he leered.

"Yeah, she is," I answered. "Not bad for a woman that mounts dead animals. But I think she's pissed at me for not giving her a tag number."

"I found mine," Rex said. "Remind me when we get back to the lodge. You can just use it."

We finished our beers and headed up the grade following Lubinski's rig.

I turned to Mike, "The only thing we don't have on this fish buy is Newt's last name."

"I was thinking about that, I'll get it from him."

"How?" I asked.

"Hide and watch, buddy," Mike said smiling.

Rex had pulled over at Snow's Rock and both he and Newt were peeing on it. We pulled in and joined them. Four fresh celebratory streams of warm, recycled Budweiser in the name of Bill Snow. A marking of an illegal fish-buy in Bill's honor.

When we pulled into the lodge, I told Lubinski we needed some fish pictures. He grabbed a long wooden rod and strung the fish through the gill plates, and we posed for photos using my camera alternating back and forth on who was snapping the images. I made sure we had several exposures with Newt and Rex. Besides the evidentiary value, I wanted to make sure we had a picture of Newt in the event we couldn't figure out his last name. Down the road, if Snow didn't recognize him, he'd know somebody who would.

I was cold and wet and headed upstairs to put on a dry set of clothes. I heard Rex's Gremlin fire up and leave. When I got to the dining room, Newt was missing and obviously he'd taken off in the car. I asked Lube about it.

"He said he had to run to 'Fino but he'll be back," Rex said and started cooking.

"Some more of that good whitetail, I hope?" Mike asked.

"Yep, this is that Christmas buck."

After dinner, I heard the Gremlin rumble in. Newt entered passing the hot tub carrying a plastic bag full of magazines. I was curious and wanted to ask but kept my mouth shut. Rex passed the obligatory Keystones around, and we moved into the living room. Newt pulled out the magazines. It was porn—not the Playboy-like stuff but hardcore porn printed on heavy glossy paper. It was nasty in-your-face crotch stuff. Newt had taken his steelhead money and spent it on pornography.

Mike popped his Keystone tab and took a swallow. "Newt, you don't need a fishing license with you when you guys are fishing do you?"

"No, we're supposed to have our tribal cards."

"A what?" Mike asked.

"A tribal card," Newt replied as he dug out a plasticized ID. He handed the card to Mike. I walked over sipping my beer and took a look at it. Newt Isaac's smiling face looked back from the card. His birth date revealed he'd turned twenty-two in November.

I spoke to Rex, "Where's that deer tag?

Rex went out to the garage and returned with a deer tag from the previous year. The tag was pristine, the month and day notches had not been cut from the tag as required by law. It was significant, no matter how Lubinski had killed the three deer from the previous fall, they were all illegal—and I wasn't including them in with the Christmas buck. I thanked him and put the tag in my wallet.

Rex must have been bored. "You guys wanna go spotlight for elk?"

"Sure," Mike answered.

Isaac passed on the offer. Apparently, he was more interested in a nice quiet night with his porn and Rex's beer.

Mike got in his rig, and I jumped into the middle. Rex took the window seat. It was another evening of driving around with a spotlight and no rifle. We drove up to the fields above the Crabtree and lit them up. There were a lot of whitetails hitting the wheat stubble along with a few elk. I thought it was a strange way to enjoy wildlife.

Mike glanced at Rex. "I'm headed straight home after this fishing trip, can you sell me some meat?"

"I can sell about ten pounds. Jimmy and I need to go hunting."

"Thirty bucks okay?"

"Works for me," Rex responded and paused. "So Donny liked the moose meat I sent down with ya, eh?"

"Yeah, he really did. And that reminds me. He can't get moose down there and wants to know if he could get a hundred pounds of it and maybe a hundred pounds of elk too if you're interested. He's wanting to do his game feed four times a year."

Rex didn't hesitate, "That shouldn't be a problem."

"Oh, and he said three bucks a pound was fine too," Mike went on shifting his gaze from over the wheel back to Lubinski, "If you could freeze it and put it in boxes wrapped in newspaper he'd pay for two-day UPS. I can give you a check for the whole nine yards the next time we come up if that's okay?"

"I can do that," Rex replied.

I could hear his smile in the darkness.

The headlights caught the eyes of a doe in front of us and Rex swiveled the light over the hood of the truck to get a better look at it. The light bouncing off the truck's hood exposed Rex's unshaven face and his longish greasy hair. He began telling us a tale. "Back in Wisconsin I used to spotlight for hunters. They'd call in their deer orders the week before the season and I'd go out and spotlight for them. One night I was on a roll. The rut was on and there was bucks everywhere. I'd shoot one and throw out a beer can to mark the spot. I'd knocked down seven decent bucks and out of nowhere a fucking warden lit me up like he was the mothership. It scared the shit out of me. It was blacker than hell out and all of a sudden there was lights everywhere. I'd no idea he'd been behind me. I got a ticket for the spotlighting but he never found any of the deer."

"Sounds like a crazy night," I said looking behind us. "I hope the bastards aren't out tonight."

"Hey," I asked. "Whatever happened to your manager, that Robert guy?"

"Oh, ...let's just say we had a little disagreement," Rex explained with a wicked chuckle.

His answer made me wonder if there weren't a fresh grave somewhere behind the Crabtree.

When we returned to the lodge Newt was still looking at his porn and drinking. Rex and Mike got several packages of moose meat out of the garage freezer and loaded them in our cooler. Mike wrote him out a check, and he and Rex carried the cooler over to the back of Mike's rig. The antlers from the Christmas buck were lying on his workbench. I turned my back on the two, pulled the camera out of my coat pocket, made sure the flash was off and quickly snapped a photo of the antlers without bringing the camera to my eye. It was risky, but I had captured evidence of the Christmas buck on film. With the photo and corroborating statements from Charbonneau and Lubinski, it was a prosecutable count. It had been a productive day.

Chapter 8

Loose Lips

The next morning Mike pulled his checkbook out to square up with Lubinski.

"My accountant wants me to separate the food out from the lodging on my expense account," Mike explained. "What do you want me to call the meals?"

"Just put it down on the check as food. That way it doesn't look like I'm cooking meals up here."

We loaded our bags and said our goodbyes.

"I'll have the two hundred pounds of meat in a couple weeks; it shouldn't be a problem. Oh, and Jimmy said if you guys want to come back next month it would be okay to go hunting with him," Lube smiled.

We drove down the grade, crossed the Clearwater, gassed up in Grangeville and called Mike's boss Roger with me listening in. Mike explained we were clear and told him about the fish and meat we'd bought, as well as the fact that Lubinski had agreed to sell us two hundred pounds of meat. He added the part about being invited to hunt with Charbonneau next month. I was standing close to Mike listening. Both of us were smiling with enthusiasm.

"How much money did you spend?" I heard Roger asking.

Mike made eye contact with me, and I watched his smile slide off his face. We had both worked our butts off, and the head of SIU seemed only to be interested in how much money we'd spent. Mike hung up.

"Bean counters," I said.

At McCall, I threw my gear in my marked vehicle and loaded the cooler full of steelhead. I volunteered to take custody of the meat that we'd bought and send samples off to the lab, and Mike took me up on the offer. The Salmon Fish and Game office had a walk-in evidence cooler and it was the obvious place to store the evidence.

The fish were going to be easy, I'd just measure them and re-bag and attach an evidence tag. They wouldn't have to be sent to the lab. One of our fish biologists could analyze a scale sample and testify in court that they were truly steelhead. The several packages of moose meat was another matter. I'd have to assign each package with an individual evidence number, start a log, thaw them without bringing them in contact, cut a sample from each, repackage the larger parent pieces, label the forensic samples with the parent evidence number and package them without exposing them to cross contamination. The process would take the better part of a day, and it was the type of work I didn't care for. However, proper evidence handling protocol could make or break a case. But it would be a good excuse to talk to Tina.

Driving along the Salmon River below Challis, I realized the ice had quit flowing in the river, and it had brought out the steelhead anglers. As I drove by I'd wave at them and they'd wave back. My boss would want me to get out and check them this week. Somehow I'd have to sell him on why I needed to work on the SIU case instead of checking fishing licenses and do it in a manner without telling him any details since he wasn't supposed to be in the loop.

In Salmon I stopped at the kennel and picked up my dog Ben and snuck him inside my state truck—once again breaking the rules. We pulled into my driveway, and I saw gravel showing through the snow. Maybe I'd get lucky and spring would come to the Salmon country early this year. I walked through my front door and turned on my message machine. Back to the uniform and away from the rolling deception of undercover work. It was good to be home with my dog and with my ball cap facing forward.

I slept in the next morning, took a long hot shower, put some civvies on and headed down to the North Fork Store in my personal Ford pickup with Ben sitting on the seat next to me. I parked and walked into the restaurant side of the building. The waitress greeted me by my first name and asked how the steelheaders were doing.

"I've been out of town and was going to ask what you'd heard."

"It sounds as if it's been slow, just typical steelhead fishing," she said filling my coffee mug.

After a quiet breakfast, I walked over to the Post Office and greeted "my" postmaster Patti. We chatted about the snow conditions while she handed me a bundle of mail that was too big for my box. I drove home, and was greeted by the steady green light on my message machine indicating I hadn't missed any calls. I laid the mail bundle on my table and went through it separating the chaff from the bills. I unpacked my gear and laid down on the couch with Salmon's weekly paper and fell asleep. The house was as messy as Lube's lodge, but I had no energy for cleaning.

Later that afternoon I called Ed to let him know I was home. I explained I had evidence that needed to be logged and shipped to the lab and another twenty or so pages of a report I needed to crank out. He understood that those things had to get done but Ed made it clear that he wanted me out checking steelheaders. I wasn't gung-ho on the species as an enforcement priority since the annual run numbers varied widely from year to year. The fluctuations were caused by changes in juvenile (downriver) migration flows along with ocean conditions. The fish needed a sensible level of protection when they returned as adults but an over emphasis of enforcement efforts wasn't going to have a measurable effect. Ed was focused on his dominion in Salmon and I was focused on what was transpiring on the Clearwater. Conflict was in the air.

I took the packages of frozen meat out of the cooler that Lubinski had sold to Mike and laid them on my kitchen counter to finish thawing. The steelhead needed to be moved to the evidence cooler in Salmon for storage but first they needed to be documented. I took them out of the cooler and laid them in the snow in the front yard, I measured and photographed them and loaded them in a heavy-duty garbage bag. I pulled an evidence tag off my truck's visor, filled out the date and description and wired it to the bag and loaded the fifty some pounds of fish in my truck bed.

I changed into my uniform; Ben caught the cue and stood up wagging his tail. We walked out the front door. I dropped the tailgate and he jumped into the bed curiously sniffing the sack of fish. I got in the driver's seat, started the engine, picked the microphone up and broadcast to no one in particular; "seven-two-five is ten-eight," and rolled out onto the highway heading for Salmon. I glanced into the mirror and Ben had settled into his dog crate. Two anglers were loading a drift boat on a trailer at the Red Rock boat ramp so I stopped, chatted with them for a bit, and checked their licenses. One of them had a fine twenty-five-inch hatchery steelie that he'd added to his permit by removing the proper notch and writing in the date and river section. They'd enjoyed their day on the river and were both energized and friendly sportsmen. It was a positive refresher for me after living and drinking with the people I had spent the last week with. The contact reminded me who was paying the tab for our Crabtree investigation.

At the office I opened up the walk-in freezer, flipped on the light and entered its macabre interior. The decapitated head of a mature bighorn ram stared at me from a shelf with iced-white pupils. Beside the sheep head lay a great horned owl and a golden eagle. On the floor lay a young frozen mountain lion in a twisted pose with a bloody icicle hanging from its ear. Several deer and elk antlers were stacked in the corner, most had been sawn off their skulls but two deer heads were still in the lot. A pair of elk hindquarters were leaning next to the antlers. Every critter part was wearing an evidence tag and they were all awaiting their hoped-for day of justice.

I took down the clipboard holding the evidence log and started to fill in the next available line: "Steelhead, 7 each, Tony Latham" and added my signature and date along with the number from the attached evidence tag. I unlocked my assigned locker labeled "725" and added the bag of fish to the other bagged and tagged items it contained. I wrote the evidence tag number down on my pocket notebook since I'd need to include it in my report for cross-referencing. I locked the door on my evidence locker, walked out and shut the freezer door turning my back on its frozen occupants. It was a wildlife morgue, and I was always struck by what it held.

When I walked in the front door, my phone started to ring. I reached to pick it up and froze. The caller ID showed a 476 prefix. *Shit,* I thought, *it's an Orofino number*, and it didn't look like Snow's. I stared at it and let it ring and ring, finally the machine answered; "This is Tony, leave a message -BEEP." A female voice followed; "Hey, this is Lisa Gardiner in Ahsahka. I need that deer tag number, give me a call."

I was glad I hadn't picked up. I didn't feel capable of jumping from Latham to Henderson at the drop of a hat especially while wearing my uniform. Maybe Mike could make the flip, but I wasn't in his league. It dawn on me that I'd have to make damn sure to look at the caller ID every time it rang.

I made a peanut butter sandwich and washed it down with a glass of milk while mentally getting in role to return her call. I sat at my desk and looked at my undercover driver's license to help with the process and thought about the persona of Henderson for a minute. My tape recorder was hard wired into the phone line. I pulled Lubinski's unvalidated deer tag out of my undercover wallet, took a deep breath, let it out, and dialed Lisa Gardiner's number. On the fifth ring, it was picked up.

"Yeah?" a husky male voice asked.

"Is the taxidermist in?"

I heard him say, "It's for you."

Followed by a pause and then, "This is Lisa."

"Yeah, this is Tony Henderson in Hailey–I've got that tag number for you."

"Good, give it to me, I'm ready."

I told her the number and then repeated it.

"Thanks, is that your number or your girlfriend's? She asked.

"It's Lubinski's, is that okay?"

"It'll work. I think you can pick your horns up next month if you're gonna be up here."

"Good, Pate and I'll be up and we'll grab it."

After she'd hung up, I clicked my phone off and listened to ensure I had a dial tone. I spoke the date and time into the line and turned the recorder off.

I rewound the tape and listened to the recording. She still sounded grouchy, but I couldn't detect any hesitation from her after I told her whose tag it was. Despite my nervousness I sounded relaxed. I felt fine about my performance

I took the following day off, picked the house up a bit, attacked my pile of dirty laundry, and found some time to relax. Although the weather was nice, I had no interest in steelhead fishing on the Salmon; I'd had enough of that in Lube's world.

The following day I started writing the report. I called Mike and told him about Lisa Gardiner and the tag. He told me he would call Lube, thank him and try to get him to talk about the pending meat deal of moose and elk for Donny. Mike would have him UPS the meat to the address and have California Fish and Game pick it up and log it as evidence.

That afternoon I took samples from each package of "M-Steak." Everything had to be numbered, labeled and logged. Each parent steak had to remain isolated and double bagged. I cut the lab samples one at a time from its parent only after putting on fresh gloves and using a new razor blade. Each sample was also isolated by double bagging to prevent cross contamination. When I was done, the kitchen garbage can was half full of slightly used latex gloves and sprinkled with once used razor blades.

At the lab, Tina would singe the exterior of each sample prior to removing tissue from inside it to further ensure the sample had not been cross contaminated. All this prior to running each item through the various tests it would take to get the desired result of forensically proving what species it came from

By the end of the week, I had the report roughed out. Ed and I had talked on the phone, and he'd asked me how many steelheaders I had checked. I didn't hedge my answer. He was not pleased. He wanted me out on the river checking anglers.

The following day I put a copy of my twenty page report in a large manila envelope and stamped it "CONFIDENTIAL" in red ink. I drove the twenty-one miles to Salmon and met with Ed. I felt I had to placate him and get him to understand why I wasn't out looking at fishing licenses.

I gave the envelope to Ed and asked him to read it and put it my inbox when he was done.

His demeanor was businesslike but he explained, "Fishermen expect to see us out working, not parked in our driveway."

Driving home I felt as though I was being accused of not working. My anger showed since I drove past several steelheaders that I should have pulled over and contacted. Ed wasn't going to win an award for motivational supervision.

A week later I bumped into my friend Merlin Guth at the grocery store in Salmon. Merlin's father Norm ran a guided steelhead jet boat business below the end of Salmon River road. Merlin had taught me how to run the department's jet boat in what we called the wilderness section of the canyon. It had taken him a week to teach me where every rock lay for thirty-plus miles that had several Class IV rapids. It had been no small effort on his part, and a huge challenge for me. He had done this for free, motivated by the fact that he and his family wanted to see a game warden in a river section that had been somewhat lawless for many years.

We chatted about steelhead fishing and then he laughed, "Hey, I understand you've been buying steelhead from the Indians."

It hit me with a hammer. I was stunned. Merlin picked up on my reaction. Maybe I'd cussed and was too upset to hear myself. Maybe it was the look on my face.

"Oops, I guess I'm not supposed to know that," he replied.

"Where did you hear that from?"

"I was ice fishing up at the lake the other day, and Ed and Brent checked me and they were laughing about it."

"Which one told you?"

Merlin must have realized that I was seeing blood and on the hunt.

He looked at me and apologized with a lowered voice, "Shit Tony, I don't really remember."

I asked Merlin if he had told anybody else about it, and he said he hadn't, and promised to keep his mouth shut. I trusted he would.

I drove back to the office and caught Ed at his desk. I shut the door and confronted him. Smoke must have been coming out of my ears, for I was burning.

He looked away from me and said, "I remember one of us saying something about it, and I guess we shouldn't have."

I picked up Ed's phone and dialed Brent up and stuck him up on it. "I can't remember if it were Ed or me that let it out, but I'll make sure and keep it quiet."

The bottom line, neither of them should have known about the investigation and it was my fault for allowing it to happen. I'd given it to my boss believing he would read it and understand why I hadn't found the time to check steelheaders and assumed he'd maintain proper need-to-know protocol and not mention it to anyone. He and Brent were good uniform officers, and both were aware of the protocol on SIU cases but neither had worked undercover. They just didn't really get it and one or both of them couldn't keep their mouths shut.

When I got home, I called Mike and told him what had happened. I had made my point to Ed, Brent, and Merlin about keeping their mouths shut but who else had they told? Mike and I had two options—either take the case down with what we had, or cross our fingers and hope the information didn't travel back to Orofino. We absolutely had Lubinski and Isaac, but we couldn't really pin anything on Charbonneau. We were certain Jimmy was trafficking and he seemed to be Lubinski's main ticket. We needed to nail him.

Mike thought about it and responded. "If it gets back to 'Fino, we'll know 'cause Rex will not ship the meat and he'll give us the cold shoulder. Let's just keep our wits about us and keep plugging away. If it smells like we've been burned we can back out and take it down."

I was still pissed but after talking about it with him I felt better. Most Salmonites had never even been to Orofino. It was a long circuitous drive to get there from Salmon. For all practical purposes the Clearwater country was in a different state. It would probably be okay, just a lesson learned.

The following week Mike called me and told me that he had talked to Lubinski. Lube had called him and said he had killed a moose with Jimmy, and would ship a hundred pounds of it to Donny. Mike suggested I call Lube up and get him to talk about killing the moose. A second corroborated statement would strengthen the case.

I put the call off that night, I was nervous; the notion felt out of character to call Lube out of the blue. The next morning I had an idea, an excuse for the call.

"Hey Rex, this is Tony in Hailey, how you doing?"

"Good, what's up?"

"I called Lisa Gardiner up and gave her your deer tag number, and she sounded kinda pissed."

"She's always bitchy; I think her husband thumps on her."

"Well that make sense, maybe you need to invite her down to the lodge," I laughed. "How's the fishing been anyway?"

"Good, and so has the hunting," he chuckled, "I got a nice two-year old bull moose with Jimmy the other day."

"Cool! Did you get it with that little twenty-two deer killing rifle?"

"No, I used my ought-six."

"Where'd you hit it?"

"Right in the fuckin' head, we was able to drive my truck right up to it."

"Sweet! Is Donny going to get some of it?"

"Yeah, it's all packaged up and ready to go."

"I gotta be in Fairbanks on the thirteenth of next month. Pate's gotta hit his accounts in Boise and I was hoping to get up there one more time before going back to work. You think the fishing's going to be any good towards the end of the month?"

"Yeah, it should be, they're catching some below the dam right now."

"That figures. I'm down here and the fish are biting. But the good news is they are already talking about detailing a bunch of us jumpers down to Boise since its been so damn dry. I went ahead and told my boss to throw my name in the hat if it happens."

"Well you and Pate should come on up before you have to take off."

After I hung up and verbally documented the date and time on the recording, I listened to the conversation twice. Rex hadn't changed, and my side of the conversation sounded fine. The recording plus the meat shipped by Lubinski to California would make a solid case for the unlawful killing and sale of moose. But Lube's word was not enough to charge Jimmy Charbonneau. We needed to go "play" with Jimmy.

Chapter 9

On Indian Time

The following day my phone rang, and I found a bright voice at the other end.

"Tony, this is Tina at the lab, I just ran your last evidence submission through the isoenzyme-typing electrophoresis protocol and you were right; the proteins all tested positive for moose."

The important part of what Tina had just told me was clear. The meat that Lubinski had sold us was moose. Beyond that, the rest was chemical mumbo-jumbo that I wasn't even going to try to understand. The other fact was that she had taken my eight evidentiary samples and run each through three individual test protocols, twenty-four tests in all, to obtain evidence that we could use in court. It was a significant amount of work that I suspected took the better part of a week.

Tina's call caused me to pause and think about the effort that had taken place with the case and what other work would be needed to bring it to a successful conclusion. Bill Snow had gained the trust of somebody to the point that they had provided information that would probably cause them harm if leaked. Roger Jones, Mike's boss, had read Bill's reports in Boise and determined that the damage to the wildlife justified committing two officers and a chunk of money from an underfunded short-handed agency. There was the work that Mike and I were putting into this beast, and now Tina at the Ashland lab had spent several days on the last batch of evidence. And I couldn't even guess what the lab's cost would be. We had yet to meet with the Clearwater County prosecutor and get him involved, but eventually he'd have to contribute a significant effort. And then there was Donny and California Fish and Game's efforts on the meat that was headed their way—it would have to be sampled, tested, and stored in a secure facility.

The phone rang again. I glanced at the caller ID and it was Mike; he must have been reading my thoughts.

"Hey buddy, you tired of this case yet?" he asked.

"Not me, why?"

"Because we're just gettin' started," he answered. "We've gotta get some charges on Charbonneau, he's our trigger man, we can't prove it yet. I'd also like to figure out who his clients are who are buying all those fish. And while I'm thinking about it, let's not forget to work on the names of Lube's kids when we get up there next week."

"I was thinking about the same thing. Those little shits of his need a spanking from the judge," I added. "By the way, the Ashland lab just called. No surprise, but that last batch of meat you bought from Lube? It's definitely moose."

"It isn't the last batch since I just got a call from Donny. He just received the hundred pounds of moose meat from Lube. Nancy from California's Special Operations Unit is headed over to pick it up right now, she'll send samples to Ashland."

"Well," I said. "Lube shipping that box to California across state lines is a good federal charge."

Mike's voice raised in pitch. "I believe Roger will let us charge Lube with a Lacey Act in federal court when it actually happens," Mike added. "For some reason he's got a piss'n match going with the local Fish and Wildlife special agent, and we need that guy to bring federal charges."

"And another thing," Mike changed the subject. "Roger handed me a report today that Snow just sent in. Bill says there's a guy from Avery by the name of Mickey White who's trading marijuana for steelhead, he's getting the fish from our buddy, Jimmy. Here, let me read it to you: 'According to warden Bill Carter, White is a real bad actor. He's a logger by trade, heavy drinker, and violent when drinking. He frequents the Logger Bar at Avery; Carter stated that White might have connections with the Aryan Nations Compound.' I won't bother to read the whole thing," Mike stated. "It goes on and on about this Mickey White guy. It sounds like he's a major dope dealer and he goes to Orofino a lot and trades dope for fish with Jimmy."

"Great," I said. "Aryan Nations, drugs, and steelhead. Maybe I can buy some Nazi collectables to go along with my butterfly knife," I laughed and then paused. "I wonder if he turns around and sells the fish in Avery?"

Mike and I discussed our pending trip. We had agreed to head back to Orofino the following Thursday, the 26th of March. We were still getting an occasional snow squall in North Fork but since Orofino was three thousand feet lower, I was hoping to see some green-up.

Steelhead fishing was nearing its end, but the season was still on so we could continue to use it for an excuse to go "play." Since we'd focused on bank-fishing on the last trip, we wouldn't have to haul the boat up.

It was our belief that Lube was trying to hook us up with a hunt with Charbonneau, so I signed out the video camera from the enforcement office in Salmon. If critters started dying, having it on video would greatly assist us in court. I went through the camera's bag as if it were a crime scene ensuring nothing in it left any tell-tale game warden signs. The camera itself had the usual green departmental property sticker on its side, just like the one Mike had found inside the drift boat; however, this sticker managed to fall into my trash contrary to state policy.

I called up Ed and reminded him I'd be leaving the following day. His voice sounded somewhat constrained, and I'm sure it was caused by the confrontation I'd had with him over the security leak. Mike had felt the need to brief his boss on the breach since it involved officer safety, and we'd both wondered if it would lead to Ed getting an ass chewing from headquarters. If it happened, it happened, but it wouldn't help my working relationship if Ed turned out to be vindictive.

The next morning I packed my bags for Orofino with Ben-dog watching me with a long face. He knew what was up. Packing for this gig was becoming rote, but I still went through each pocket to make sure nothing had migrated that would give us up. I'd used my daypack on a foot patrol and made sure it was clean and my snubbed nosed .38 was loaded and stashed in its hidey-hole. I dropped Ben off at the kennel, stopped at my bank and withdrew $200 in twenties from my personal account to cover any unforeseen purchases. The cash went in my undercover wallet and the receipt with my real name on it went in the wooden box on my truck seat. I was beginning to get paranoid concerning the security on this case but didn't think it was a bad idea. The department would reimburse me if I needed the money for something like steelhead, but I would have to write an affidavit stating what the item was purchased for and why I couldn't get a receipt for it. The system was cumbersome, a pain in the ass, but a necessary part of covert work.

From the bank, I headed to the sheriff's dispatch office. One thing that was bugging me about the case was how Jimmy Charbonneau was getting around. The night Lubinski took us to his camper, there was no vehicle. Since Jimmy was always drinking, I questioned whether he had a valid driver's license.

I entered the dispatch office through the back door. I nodded at the dispatcher and helped myself to the ever-present coffee carafe. Bill Inman was seated looking at two computer monitors and was wearing a headset. He was apparently talking with someone on the phone. When he was done I greeted him, handed him a piece of paper with Jimmy Charbonneau's name and date of birth on it and asked him to run him for a driver's license and vehicle registrations.

After a few seconds Bill dropped his chin and looked over his reading glasses at me and said, "I can't find a driver's license for this guy; let me see what he's got for vehicles."

I sipped away as Inman inputted Charbonneau's information into the data fields.

"Nothing, nada, not a thing. You want me to run him in another state?"

"Nope, he's an Idaho boy, but thanks."

Jimmy Charbonneau was 47 years old. He'd apparently been born and raised in the Orofino area, presumably living there his entire life and there was no record of him having had a driver's license. And seemingly he had not owned any vehicles in the last several years, probably never. It offered a curious insight into the man, but it didn't answer the nagging question of how he got around.

I met Mike at the McCall Hatchery, stowed my gear inside his camper shell and we headed north towards Orofino. We went over what both of us felt needed to get accomplished on this trip. He'd talked to Snow about setting up a covert meeting with the prosecutor. Snow had called back, and the county had a trial scheduled. We'd have to put the meeting off for now. The conversation shifted to Jimmy Charbonneau; we really didn't have much predisposition on him. Jimmy had admitted giving elk and moose to some guy in California, had talked about bartering fish for dope, and hunting illegally with non-tribal members but we hadn't gotten anything from him in the way of serious trafficking. We still needed to get the full names of Lubinski's kids and where they lived since down the trail there would be Wisconsin game wardens knocking on their doors. And

there were "my" antlers we'd dropped off at Lisa
Gardiner's taxidermy. We'd need to pay her and pick
them up. But the main goal we'd agreed to was: Get into
Jimmy Charbonneau.

Mike glanced at me as we turned onto the highway.
"I'd really like to take this case to the point that we could
arrest some of the clients too. It's the money that's
driving this. The buyers need to be hammered along with
Charbonneau and Lubinski. If we don't stop the market,
somebody else will pick up behind these two pricks,"
Mike asserted.

We dropped off the Camas Prairie and into the
Clearwater. The canyon was in full green-up and smelled
earthy. The main Clearwater was running some color,
Orofino hadn't changed, and nobody had stolen Snow's
Rock. It was almost good to be back.

The first thing I noticed at the Crabtree was the K-car
parked out front that had belonged to Lubinski's
manager, Robert Deacon. I was really curious to see
whether Robert was in the Crabtree since the last thing
Lube had said about him left me wondering if he hadn't
done him in.

Rex met us at the door. He hadn't changed, his smile
was still missing a tooth and he looked as though he
needed a good scrubbing. As usual, his right hand held a
Keystone, and he invited us in. We sat down in the living
room, and he pulled a couple more beers out of the
refrigerator for us.

"What you been up to, buddy?" Mike asked.

"Well, mostly hunting, but it's been poor," Rex said, "Jimmy and I went out a couple of days ago and he wounded an elk."

"Can't that Indian hit anything?" Mike asked.

"Yeah, he's normally real good, he likes shooting 'em in the head most of the time just like me. I shot that fuckin' moose in the head two weeks ago and it went right down," Rex spouted.

"Jimmy sounds as if he shoots like your boys," Mike laughed. "You need to teach them how to shoot. They coming back this spring?"

"Naw, they've got jobs, I'll get them back here this next winter to hunt."

"Have you got any pictures of 'em?" Mike asked.

Lubinski walked over to a bookshelf, pulled a photo album down, and took it over to Mike.

"This one is Jerry, he lives in Watertown. This is my other son Larry, he lives in Menomonee."

I walked over to look, Lube was showing us a photograph of two guys in their twenties with two dead cow elk in the back of his Dodge pickup truck. Both were smiling. They looked like Lube. The same beards and hair–just twenty years younger. Another generation of wildlife thieves.

"Are those the elk they got this winter?" Mike asked.

"Yeah, you betcha, they ain't that bad of shots," Rex laughed.

Lubinski had just handed us his two boys on a platter. At the end of the covert portion of the investigation, we would have a raid team serve a search warrant on the Crabtree and recover the photos.

"How's business been here?" Mike asked.

"I had a couple last week from Spokane; they were visiting some relatives around here for a few days."

"You show a profit with this place with the IRS?" Mike queried.

"Hell no, I don't pay motel taxes or sales tax or nothing, I don't believe in that shit," Rex ranted. "I just deny doing any business."

"How's Jimmy been?" Mike asked.

Rex lowered his voice, "He's really been drinking hard but he's been selling a lot of fish too."

"Is he still not eating anything?" I asked. "How does he even live?"

"He just drinks a lot a beer; it's how he gets his grub I guess."

"How's the fishing been?" I asked.

"Its kinda slowed down except right at the hatchery," he replied.

"Donny loved that moose meat. I'd bet he'll take another hundred pounds. And he still wants some elk," Mike threw out.

"Good," Rex responded. "I was wondering about that. We should be able to come up with an elk soon, hopefully this week. You guys should fish tomorrow morning," Rex suggested. "I'll get Jimmy later, and we'll all go hunting in the afternoon."

"Sounds good," Mike answered. "Have you got that UPS receipt? I'll give you a check for it and the meat."

"Yeah, I got it right here."

Lubinski pulled a brown and white piece of paper from a pile of papers on the kitchen counter and handed it to Mike.

"This'll make my accountant happy," Mike explained.

Mike wrote out a check for $450 and handed it to Rex. "Three hundred for the meat and a hundred and fifty for the shipping," Mike explained and slipped the UPS receipt into his shirt pocket.

He and Rex were beaming. Lube had just caught a wad of money and Mike had just gotten the proof that Lube had actually been the one to ship the meat.

Robert Deacon walked down the staircase; he was wearing John Lennon wire-rims and looked as though he'd just woken up. He nodded at us and lit a cigarette. He took some food out of the refrigerator and pulled a frying pan off the wall. *So much for an undercover homicide investigation,* I thought to myself.

We had a dinner of whitetail and fried potatoes washed down by Rex's cheap beer. Robert and Lube acted as if each other didn't exist. It was obvious they weren't best buddies but for whatever reason they were back together. Mike and I called it an early night and headed to bed.

The next morning we found Rex sitting alone at the table drinking coffee. Robert was no place to be seen. I poured a couple of cups for Mike and I, and we sat down.

"Rex," Mike said, "This place is a dammed pigsty. You need to get somebody to come in and do some cleaning."

"Jeez," Rex whined, "Yous guys is like family now so don't be saying that shit."

The place *was* dirty. It made my bachelor's pad at home look like a nunnery. His floor was filthy, an open newspaper was scattered about; empty beer cans and ashtrays full of cigarettes adorned the coffee table in the living room. I felt Lube getting pissed and changed the subject.

"I thought you and Robert had a falling out?" I asked.

"Yeah, but we kissed and made up," Rex sniggered.

Lubinski cooked us a breakfast of eggs, sausages, and leftover potatoes.

"I'll find Jimmy this afternoon and we'll see if we can't find Donny an elk," Rex said smiling.

"If you find him we'll be up by the dam," Mike replied.

Mike and I headed out to fish—or at least look as if we were fishing. We drove down the grade and turned back up the North Fork to the dam. The sun was breaking through the cloud cover and illuminating the fresh green-up across the river. There were few anglers along the bank, and it told me the fishing was about over for the spring. Any steelhead still around were probably stacked up below the hatchery. We parked Mike's rig and went through the motions of baiting up and casting. The sun felt warm and the place smelled simple and spring like. It was an enjoyable but boring morning.

After three hours of casting and feeling our sinkers dragging over the river's bottom, we drove down to grab a burger at the Woodlot. Lubinski had not talked of any specific time or place and I wondered if the hunt would come together like his whorehouse plans.

We finished up our burgers and drove onto the bridge towards Orofino. I looked down at a group of people standing by the outlet of the hatchery and saw the unmistakable profile of big Jimmy Charbonneau. He was perched on a granite rock the size of a Volkswagen. Another half-dozen Indians with poles were standing near him on the riverbank.

Mike pulled into the parking lot, and we walked down along the ditch-like raceway that led from the hatchery to the river. I felt as if we were walking into enemy territory.

About half the Indians fishing looked heavy and the other half looked skinny. Jimmy had a hundred pounds over the next largest and looked as though he was wearing the same dirty clothes from last month. He had his signature black ball-cap on backwards and had a large cream colored fishing pole held by his massive left hand. His fingers looked like hot dogs wrapped around the pole's handle.

"Hey Jimmy, how's the fishing?" Mike asked.

Jimmy looked up. "I'm gettin' a few," he said and gave a nudge to a wet lumpy burlap bag laying next to him with his boot. A fish flopped in the bag, still half alive.

Jimmy reeled in. I could see a wicked looking two-inch treble hook on the end of his heavy monofilament. A large chunk of lead was molded onto the hook's shank. He cast the rig back in, let it sink for a moment and gave a quick jerk to the rod, then reeled the slack in and jerked again. The other tribal members around him were using the same jerking and reeling snagging technique. I heard an Indian say something unintelligible. I glanced over and he had a fish on. He pulled the steelhead to the top. A big treble hook was impaled midway into the fish's back. The Indian jerked the yard-long fish across the surface and up onto the bank. He dragged the flopping fish up through the boulders, picked up a softball sized rock and smashed its head. The fish convulsed and sprayed eggs from its vent.

I turned back to Charbonneau and asked, "How many you get this winter?"

"About three-hundred, maybe three-fifty. It's been a slow year, I normally catch five or six hundred."

"Oh, bullshit," exclaimed Lubinski.

I turned around, and Lube's tooth-missing smile greeted us, his right hand grasp an open Keystone, his left hand held an empty plastic loop with three dangling beers. He passed the half-six-pack to me, I took a beer and handed the remaining two to Jimmy; he passed the leftover to Mike.

"How about we all go hunting, Jimmy?" Rex asked.

Jimmy looked at his fish sack and said, "Come pick me up in 'bout an hour or so, I ain't ready yet."

Lubinski swallowed what was left of his beer and threw the can in the rocks. I looked at my watch and noted it was 1:57 for my future report. The three of us left Jimmy and walked back to the parking lot.

"We're running on Indian time now," Rex said. "I'll try to get him up to the lodge in a few hours and we can go hunt."

Chapter 10

The Dying Quivers

Rex got in his rig, and Mike and I got in ours. We followed his Dodge out of the parking lot. He turned right to Orofino, and we turned left towards the Crabtree. Mike and I talked about what to do, assuming it all came to together; we had at least an hour to kill before Rex brought Jimmy up.

Mike looked over at me. "Let's just go back to the lodge, Rex's cowboy hat is probably lying around and we can photograph the eagle feather."

When we got back to the Crabtree, Robert's K-car was parked closer to the entrance. We walked in; Robert was sitting at the couch smoking a cigarette and drinking a beer with a heavyset blonde woman doing the same.

"Hey guys," Robert said. "This is Carol, my girlfriend."

Mike and I introduced ourselves.

A young girl walked down the stairs with an older high-school age boy. The boy looked at me and nodded agreeably before the two disappeared out the door.

"That's my daughter Trudy and her boyfriend Adrian," Carol said.

The girl looked much too young to have a boyfriend but at least he looked like a nice kid.

"She go to school in 'Fino?" I asked.

"Yeah, she's just finishing up ninth grade."

Mike and I headed up to our room. He sat down on a dumpy sofa and I lay down on my bed and we talked quietly. I didn't have any children, but I was surprised a mother would allow a fourteen-year old to have a boyfriend. *She just looks like a kid*, I thought.

"Pate," I said to Mike, "How long before you let your daughters start dating? Aren't they about the same age as that girl out there?"

"Yeah, but if it's up to me, they can't start dating until they're thirty."

The next thing I heard Mike say was, "Hey, wake up Henderson, we're going hunting."

I followed Mike down the stairs feeling groggy. Rex was in the living room wearing his cowboy hat and talking with Robert. He turned and said, "Let's go huntin'."

"Did you get Jimmy?" I asked.

"Yeah, he's out front."

"We can take my rig," Mike offered.

I went outside, Jimmy was standing next to Rex's Dodge with a scoped bolt-action rifle and a double bitted axe laying across the hood.

"What ya shooting there, Jimmy?"

"Two-forty-three, it kicks like a twenty-two but punches like an ought-six."

"Winchester?"

"No, it's a Remington," he answered.

My daypack was in the front of Mike's truck; I grabbed it and the video camera bag and put them inside the bed under the canopy. A big well-used nylon rope was in the truck bed that I hadn't seen before. Rex and I crawled into the back of the truck, and I closed the canopy door. He had a .22 rifle and a .357 revolver in a leather gun belt lying beside him. Mike and Jimmy got in the cab.

I turned to Rex, "Is this your rope?"

"No, it's Jimmy's."

We drove down the grade and into Orofino. Mike pulled into the IGA grocery store and got out walking towards the store's entrance.

"Where you going?" I asked through the screen.

"Jimmy needs some beer."

A few minutes later Mike walked out carrying a red case of Budweiser. He stopped at the tailgate and handed a couple of cans to me. I gave one to Rex and opened the other. Driving around with Rex Lubinski in the back of a truck drinking beer would have normally been the last thing I wanted to do, but this trip held promise.

We turned up the Wells Bench Road and drove through conifers and farm fields. We crossed a bridge over an arm of the reservoir. I looked out the window at the lowering sun and asked Rex where we were headed.

"Swamp Creek."

"Does this bridge have a name?"

"Yeah, it's Dent's Bridge," he answered.

Across the reservoir, we entered a thick forest with interspersed clear-cuts. It was mostly Douglas fir and larch with a few red cedar trees. Undeniably it was logging country. The clear-cuts were thick with brush and young evergreens were starting to push up. We'd climbed two thousand feet above the Clearwater and lost most of the green-up. The brush hadn't leafed out yet, but the air had the smell of earth and spring. If it weren't for the company, I was with it would have been a fine evening for a drive.

Mike slowed down for a junction and turned right. I looked out, and caught a glimpse of a Forest Service sign telling us we had just turned off the Elk River Road and were headed to Swamp Creek.

"This is some wild-ass looking country," I said.

"Yeah it's full of game and there shouldn't be anybody out here tonight."

"You bring your kids up here last month?"

"As a matter of fact I did. They got both their elk a couple of miles out this road."

"Have they gotten elk before?"

"No this was their first. They've killed a lot of deer back in Wisconsin, though."

"I think it's pretty cool you could get 'em out here hunting with Jimmy," I told him. "I'll bet they'll remember it for the rest of their lives."

Rex smiled back at me, and I was smiling too. However, my twinkle was caused by the vision of Wisconsin wardens knocking on their doors.

Mike stopped the truck next to a clear-cut. I could see elk moving through the brush on the hillside, I pushed open the canopy's door and crawled over the tailgate. Rex followed me out. I grabbed the video camera and got it rolling expecting to hear the blast of a rifle shot. Jimmy and Mike were on the right side of the truck, and Jimmy was pointing up on the hill; his rifle held beside him by his free hand.

"There's some elk up on the hill, Rex," Jimmy said turning towards us.

"I can't see 'em," Mike complained.

Rex stepped to the other side of Mike and started pointing with his beer up on the hill.

"They's right up there," Rex directed.

"Let me use your scope," Mike said. "I can't see the dang things." Mike brought Jimmy's rifle up to his shoulder and looked through the scope.

"Are you gonna shoot?" I asked.

"Jimmy says it's too far to shoot," Mike answered. "Besides, I can't find them in the dang scope," he added.

"It's only a couple hundred yards," Jimmy said, still trying to point out the elk for Mike. "Too far to drag 'em though, the rope won't reach that far."

There were about fifteen head of cows and half-grown calves angling towards the safety of the ridge-line at a fast walk. I could see bits and pieces of brown bodies and legs through gaps in the brush. Obviously, Charbonneau had no interest in killing an elk that was beyond the reach of his rope.

When the elk disappeared, Mike and Jimmy got in the front of the truck and Rex and I resumed our places in the back.

We continued up the road. I had not seen another vehicle since we'd crossed Dent Bridge. Five minutes after the elk, Mike slowed down and stopped again. Jimmy turned back and looked at us through the cab's rear window and pointed off to the left of the truck. I looked and saw a ruffed grouse bobbing next to the road. Rex and I climbed out and this time he had his .22 rifle with him. He moved to the left side of the truck just off the bumper, and I got the video rolling behind him. He brought the gun up to shoot. I hoped like hell that Mike didn't open his door and step into the line of fire. Rex shot and killed the grouse with the camera rolling. He walked over and picked up the flopping bird.

"Hold him up for the camera," I requested.

Lubinski obliged and grinned back. He held up both arms in victory with the bird still flapping its wings. His rifle was in one hand and the bird in the other. It was a great chunk of evidence for three misdemeanors: Shooting from the road, killing a game bird during closed-season, all capped off with the illegal eagle feather stuck in his hat.

Mike had remained in his seat, and Jimmy was out peeing on the road. Rex handed the bird through Mike's open window, turned around and pointed the rifle into the brush with one hand like a pistol and fired. He looked into my camera and explained, "I don't like having a round in the chamber when I'm hunting; it ain't safe," Rex said and turned back to Mike. "Pate, can I get another Bud from ya?"

Mike handed him his second beer out the driver's window, and we walked back to the tailgate. I climbed in first, and he handed me his rifle. He shut the canopy door and I felt the truck settle as Jimmy retook his seat. Mike started the truck, and we continued toward Swamp Creek.

A few miles up the road, Mike stopped and turned off the truck. I heard him Jimmy holler back, "Hey, Rex, there's another grouse down there."

Rex and I crawled out of the back. Jimmy was pointing at a grouse standing on an old skid road about sixty yards below us on the right. Rex shot at the bird while standing on the road. It failed to react but a follow-up shot got the bird to jump.

"What ever happened to one-shot meat-in-the-pot Lubinski?" I laughed.

"Goddamned grouse!" Rex said. "Where am I hitting?" And he fired again.

"Right above him," I answered.

"Give me that damned thing," Mike said.

Rex handed the rifle to him, and Mike brought it up to his shoulder, paused, and fired a shot that struck a foot to the bird's left. His well placed bullet had finally told it to flee, and it took off at a run and disappeared into the brush. Lubinski took the rifle back and fired several times into the bushes where the bird had disappeared and laughed. We all laughed with him and got back in the truck. I was laughing since I had just gotten him on tape committing two more misdemeanors. But we still had nothing on Charbonneau.

An old snow drift blocked our descent into Swamp Creek. Mike turned around and started driving back to the Elk River Road. It was getting dark but still light enough to look into the clear-cuts for elk and deer. After a bit, Mike turned on his headlights and Jimmy started lighting up the clear-cuts with Lubinski's hand held spotlight.

Fifteen minutes into shining, the truck slowed and turned off to the right coming to a stop with the headlights shining onto the edge of a clear-cut. It was obvious Mike and Jimmy were looking at something, but Rex and I couldn't see squat from the back.

Jimmy's rifle thundered from the passenger's window, and I heard Mike, "Good shot, Jimmy."

Rex and I got out of the back of the truck. I got the tape rolling and followed Rex up through the clear-cut. He had his gun belt over his shoulder, and his .357 revolver gripped in his right hand; his other hand carried his trusted beer. Jimmy illuminated a downed doe with the spotlight that was lying next to a cedar stump. Rex walked up to it and aggressively kicked its head several times. There was no life left other than the spasms of its legs. It needed no mercy from Rex's pistol.

Mike and Jimmy got out of the truck and walked up to us. Mike was holding the cordless spotlight. He swept the scene and night-blinded me. I could hear Jimmy's labored breathing coming up the hill towards me, he was in horrible shape. *Is this guy going to have a heart attack on us?* I wondered.

The hulk of Jimmy walked up to the deer carrying a short double-bitted axe and he threw it down next to the doe.

"Where'd you hit it?" I asked.

"Right in the fuckin' head," Rex answered. "It's mush."

"Who wants the dying quivers?" Jimmy smirked.

I responded back with a low conspiratorial laugh, but I had a strange sense that he wasn't joking. He gave me a queer look when he saw I was video taping, it was obvious he didn't like it. I juggled the decision of stopping or continuing the filming. The investigator in me won out, and I kept rolling.

"We can make a movie on how to gut a deer in three minutes or less," I offered.

This egotistic suggestion seemed to put Charbonneau at ease a bit; he produced a large folding knife and sharpening steel and touched the blade up in an obvious show that he was getting ready to do his thing.

Rex grabbed a hind leg, Jimmy took the other one, and pulled the legs apart. Jimmy stepped between the legs, bent over and went to work. His blade exposed the guts and continued up through the rib cartilage along the sternum to the animal's neck. He stepped back to the animals rear, grabbed the axe, chipped at the pelvis, and then lifted it onto his knee. He pushed down on both legs and broke the pelvis open with a crunching snap.

"Jimmy," Mike said. "I see you've never done this before."

"Once or twice."

"You learn that in a book?" I added.

I had eviscerated numerous big game animals as a hunter and conservation officer but had *never* seen an animal opened up so quickly. Jimmy Charbonneau was slick with a knife, and I felt that he was showing off for the camera.

He stepped over to the steaming pile of guts, found the heart and poked into it with his knife blade. He reached down with his other hand and stuck a finger into the fresh knife hole. He raised the wet organ up by his finger and made one quick slice that severed the tissue connecting it to the rest of the gut pile. Jimmy rose up wheezing for air and stuck the heart in a plastic bag.

"What are you puffing for, boy?" Rex asked.

"I'm thirty-nine," Jimmy managed to chuckle between gasps.

"We all were once," I laughed.

Rex slid the doe down to the truck and we threw it onto the open tailgate. I helped him push it deeper into the bed, and we climbed behind the steaming carcass. I closed the canopy door, and we were blanketed by the odor of the fresh kill.

Mike started the pickup, and we headed back towards the reservoir. Jimmy ran the spotlight out his open window. The light illuminated a deer standing thirty yards off the road. Mike stopped the truck. Lubinski levered a round into the chamber of his rifle and aimed at the animal from inside the canopy. His muzzle was inches away from the window screen. The animal jumped away. Rex cussed and lowered the rifle and I heard him click the safety back on.

"It ain't legal for us to hunt with Jimmy, but as far as I can tell, there is nothing that says we can't be with him when he's just transporting game. If we get stopped tonight, we'll just tell 'em we picked him and the deer up back in here."

"That sounds good to me," I replied.

"Someday I'll probably get caught," he commiserated.

I mentally agreed with his clairvoyance.

Just before Dent, Jimmy turned the spotlight off. We were moving at forty or fifty miles an hour on the paved road. Rex opened the canopy door, stuck the muzzle out and discharged it into the blackness without a clue what lay in his line of fire. It was about the stupidest thing I had ever seen anyone do with a firearm. Had I known what he had been up to, I would have interceded but there was no calling a bullet back.

We drove down the Wells Bench Road and into Orofino. When we hit the Clearwater, Mike turned towards Ahsahka. We passed the hatchery, crossed the North Fork and headed up the grade. Mike pulled over at the Bill Snow Rock and all four of us got out and peed on the rock. The ritual was conducted without the normal banter, since we were tired. Mike managed to make eye contact with me, and his face was wearing a mischievous smirk.

It was close to midnight when we pulled into the Crabtree. Mike backed up to Lube's garage, we slid the doe out and hung it by its hind legs. Rex pulled the overhead door down and grabbed the nearly empty case of beer from Mike's truck. Jimmy and Rex walked into the lodge, and Mike and I stayed outside.

"Pate, I gotta pee like a moose," I told him.

The two of us walked to the edge of the trees where we could watch the lodge and ensure no one came out.

"What did Jimmy tell you in the cab?"

"He told me he sells steelhead for ten dollars and salmon for twenty. He also talked about taking Lube's two boys elk hunting and about the elk they killed."

"Just that? All the way out to Swamp Creek and back, and that's all he said?"

"Hell no, he said he got caught in the undercover operation selling steelhead 'cause Snow sicked them on him. He said he smelled a rat when they wanted to give him a check for the fish. I'll tell you more later."

We went inside, grabbed a couple of beers out of the open box and sat down with our two miscreants.

Rex addressed Jimmy, "You mind taking these guys hunting tomorrow? I gotta get some things done in town, and we still gotta get Donny that elk meat, eh?"

"Yeah that would be okay," he turned to Mike. "How about we leave about five?"

We agreed to the early start. I headed upstairs, stripped down and jumped in the shower. I was dirty, tired and hungry. At least I would go to bed clean.

Chapter 11

Burned

I closed my eyes and awoke with my watch alarm going off.

"Hey Pate, get your old butt up," I said. "Time to go hunting."

Mike groaned back, "Hey buddy, you're kidding me, right?"

I threw my clothes on and headed downstairs hoping that Lubinski had gotten up and made us a pot of coffee. Jimmy was sitting at the table drinking a Keystone.

"Morning Jimmy, how long you been up?"

"Just long enough to open up a beer."

I looked in the cabinet above Lube's coffee pot and found what I needed, a can of ground coffee. I pulled it and a filter down and loaded the coffee maker.

There was a loaf of white bread on the counter. I really didn't like white bread, but I was starving so I pulled out two slices and put them in the toaster. I looked in the refrigerator for some margarine or butter and came up empty but found some grape jelly. *This is sure a funky bed and breakfast,* I thought.

Mike came down the stairs looking tired.

"You want some toast, Pate?" I asked.

"Yeah, I'm dying."

"How about you Jimmy, toast?" I added

"No, I've got my breakfast right here," and took another drink.

"Morning Jimmy," Mike said. "Why ain't you drinking that Budweiser? I bought that stuff for you, man."

"It's too good to drink for breakfast."

"It's yours, Jimmy," Mike explained. "Bring it along this morning if you want."

I handed a jellied slice of toast to Mike. I pulled the half-full coffee pot from its hot plate and caught most of the trickle of hot coffee coming down from the filter with my mug leaving a puddle. I poured Mike a full mug from the pot, topped my cup off with it and switched the now empty pot back to its place under the machine. I'd made a mess, but I needed coffee. Jimmy and I had our addictions.

I slathered jelly on the two freshly toasted slices, and we headed out the door with me wolfing down the toasted sandwich and trying hard not to spill my coffee. I climbed in the middle of the truck seat and scooted over next to Mike. I set my coffee on the dash and held Jimmy's rifle as he moved in beside me and set the box of Bud on the floor. The bench seat really wasn't big enough for the three of us with Jimmy's mass, but he managed to get the passenger door closed. He reached down and retrieved a fresh Budweiser, popped the top, and took a deep drink. His rifle was held butt down on the floor with the barrel straight up. I looked down at the rifle's action trying to see whether the bolt's striker was cocked, but his big arm was in the way. I hoped the rifle had an empty chamber. What I *could* see was dried blood on his hands from last night's kill.

At the end of Rex's driveway, Jimmy told Mike to turn right.

"Where we headed?" I asked.

"I thought we'd go above Cavendish."

The road climbed above the darkened river canyon. The country started to flatten out and we passed a group of grain elevators at a junction.

"This is Cavendish," Jimmy explained. "Keep going straight. Let's go on up to Three Bears."

We had been driving through open farmland country with the first signs of morning light breaking to the east. Two whitetails leaped across the road, and Mike slammed on the brakes spilling some of my coffee.

"No," Jimmy instructed. "Let's get us a moose or elk."

"You want the spotlight?" I asked, turning to Jimmy.

"No, it'll be light when we get to some good hunting country."

The road started to cut through timbered ground, breaking back and forth from farmland to forest and finally just black timber.

It was beginning to get light enough to see game when we started to drop down into a drainage. Mike slowed down, and the three of us looked hard into each passing clear-cut. Jimmy smashed his beer can with his hands, put it back in the beer box and brought out another fresh beer.

I turned and smiled at him, "You like that Bud better than Keystone?"

"You betcha, but it costs too damn much," he laughed as he opened it up.

"What crick is this?" I asked.

"Three Bears," he said and added a belch.

We continued dropping down the drainage, the sun was breaking above the eastern skyline and lighting up the hillside on our left.

"There's an elk," Mike said and stopped the truck.

Jimmy quietly opened his door and eased his torso outside. The elk was about eighty yards above us on Mike's side, standing on a contouring skid road in the middle of a clear-cut. I grabbed the video camera off the dash, fired it up and started videoing from inside. Jimmy took up a left handed shooting position leaning across the hood, his cheek jowl tight on the far side of the stock. His black ball cap was turned backwards, and his left eye stared big into the scope. He fired and the elk started moving up the hill. Jimmy racked the rifle's bolt chambering a fresh round, he let out two soft whistles and the elk stopped for a brief moment and stared back. It was her final look, his rifle barked and she collapsed.

I looked at my watch. "Six-thirteen," I said with the camera still running.

"Good shot Jimmy," Mike said.

"It's on that skid road up there, if'n we go back up a bit we can get on it and drive right to it, maybe," Jimmy replied.

We squeezed back into the rig. Jimmy's beer had spilled on the floor, he reached back into the box and pulled out what I hoped was the last beer. Mike turned around and drove a couple of hundred yards and found the connecting road that led out across the clear-cut. The elk lay dead on the edge of the road. Jimmy and I got out while Mike found a place to turn around.

Jimmy pulled out his folding knife from of his pocket, let out a beer burp, and opened the bloodstained blade. He reached down and grabbed the cow's head by its nose and began removing the two "ivory" teeth from the upper jaw.

"How much do you get for 'em up here?" I asked filming.

"Not much, maybe five bucks."

Within a few seconds, he had the teeth out, wiped them off on his jeans, gave them a quick look, and pocketed them. I had *never* seen elk ivories removed so quickly. He followed up the extraction by cutting an incision behind the elk's head to the spine. He picked up his double bitted axe and chopped through the vertebrae spattering his face with freckles of blood. He pulled the head away from the carcass and flopped it over feeling around the smashed skull with his thumb. "That first one got her in the lower jaw, the second hit right where I was aiming."

"Never had a chance," Mike said.

Jimmy moved to the rear of the elk, lifted a leg, and leaned against it exposing its belly. He cut through the skin from the crotch up to the sternum.

"Looks like a bull got her," Jimmy said.

"She's pregnant?" I asked.

"Yeah," he replied, flopping his hand on the exposed amniotic sac and moving his cutting efforts to the cow's pelvis.

"How many elk you think you killed with that gun?" I asked.

"I couldn't count," he replied. "It's the third year with it."

Charbonneau split the chest open by axing through the sternum, he reached in and cut the esophagus and windpipe and finished the evisceration process by pulling the organs out in one big pile.

I pulled out my pocketknife and opened up the sack containing the unborn calf.

I stared down at the little wet pitiful form. "Its got spots on it and everything," I said.

"That's like looking at a human being for God's sake," Mike said disgustedly.

Jimmy picked up the steaming guts and threw them on top of the wet fetus. His reaction to Mike's revulsion surprised me, I decided he didn't share the empathy for the calf that Mike and I had.

The three of us managed to load the elk in the truck's bed under the canopy. What struck me about the loading effort was that although Charbonneau was horribly obese and out of shape, he was strong.

"Should we pay you or Rex?" Mike asked.

"Me."

We drove out of the clear-cut and got back on the graveled road heading for Cavendish.

"You guys need to know there's an undercover sting in the area buying steelhead right now," Jimmy said staring straight ahead.

I froze. He'd said it with a lowered voice. Jimmy had his rifle pointed barrel up, and I had no idea if he'd chambered a fresh round. It would be easy for his left arm to push the muzzle into my chest and pull the trigger with his right. For a moment, the silence in the cab was strangling.

"How'd you hear that?" Mike asked.

"It's going around," Jimmy replied. "I got caught in one a couple of years ago and got off even though I sold over four hundred fish to the bastard."

I was still too dumbstruck to respond. My mind was buzzing at warp speed over what he'd said. Had my boss's leak somehow made it clear across Idaho to Orofino? I mentally ran through the names of everybody who knew what we'd been up to. I absolutely trusted Bill Snow and Dave Cadwallader. Besides, Dave didn't know we'd bought fish; he just knew we were working in the area and had something involving a moose. Could it have come from the biologist Bill Atkinson whom we'd turned the meat sample over to in February? He'd mentioned tribal members were selling fish. I flashed back to my boss. It almost had to have come from his leak, he'd told Merlin I was "buying fish from the Indians." I thought about what Jimmy had said. He'd made it sound as if he'd heard something in the wind. But maybe something had hinked him up and he'd just thrown it out to see how we reacted? But one way or the other it was a bad deal. I was glad Mike had found something to say to break the silence.

The trip back to Lubinski's seemed to take a week. When we finally got to the lodge Jimmy suggested we pull around to the back side and hang the carcass under the carport. The overhang had a small block and tackle wired to a doubled 2 x 10 beam. Mike backed under it, and I got out and dropped the tailgate. Jimmy retrieved a heavy meat gambrel and a block and tackle from the garage. Lubinski appeared from around the front of the truck.

"Jeeze," Rex remarked looking at the cow. "Yous guys got a fine piece of meat there."

"Yep, old deadeye Jimmy," I managed to say wondering if I were stuttering.

"Yeah," Mike said. "But we can't find us a moose; Donny wants more moose too." I thought I caught a quiver in his voice.

"This is good," Rex said. "I'll let her hang for a week and get it deboned and frozen and then I'll get a hundred pounds boxed up and shipped down."

"That'd be great, my man," Mike replied.

Jimmy pulled his big folding knife out and flicked the blade open one-handed with his thumb. He grabbed the hind legs and cut through the skin between the tibia bones and the Achilles' tendons. He spread the legs, stuck the gambrel hooks into the cuts and attached it to the bottom of the block's pulleys. Rex and Jimmy hauled the carcass up with the block's rope and tied it off. It looked as if the effort had been rehearsed.

"Let's cook up some food, Rex," Mike exclaimed. I'm starving."

My partner's demeanor was *much* cooler than mine. I still couldn't stop thinking about what Charbonneau had said. Unless he was just on a fishing expedition, *we'd been burned and were in deep shit*; I had to assume Mike was thinking the same. We walked into the lodge, and I was grateful the big Indian left his rifle in the truck.

I helped myself to Rex's coffee pot, poured two mugs and handed one to Mike. The last thing I needed was caffeine, but I needed to be doing something and sipping coffee was about all I figured I could handle. Jimmy helped himself to a Keystone. Rex pulled a Styrofoam box of eggs out of the refrigerator and a bloody package of game meat. He took a cast iron skillet out of the sink and began cooking up a meal for the four of us. Or at least the three of us that ate solid food.

"I'll go start skinning while you guys eat," Jimmy offered and went out the back door with his beer.

Things *appeared* to be okay. Rex sounded normal; Jimmy had dropped the subject and in rethinking it, he hadn't actually accused us of being undercovers. I tried to come up with something natural to say to Lubinski and brought up the other issue that was bothering me.

"How many elk you think Jimmy has gotten with that two-forty-three of his?" I asked Rex.

"He kills about thirty a year, and he's had the rifle for three years, so it's about a hundred."

"How in the hell did you come up with thirty?"

"He told me that, and he brought at least twelve of them through here last year; I don't think he's bullshittin'."

I sipped some coffee and did a quick mental calculation; I knew that you'd get 150 to 250 pounds of meat from an elk. Using a rough average of 200 pounds of meat per elk it meant that Charbonneau was going through about 6,000 pounds of elk meat a year. I loved elk hunting (not this shoot from the road stuff) and when I put one in the freezer it would take about eighteen months for me to eat. The only thing I'd seen Jimmy eat was beer. I could only come up with two possible conclusions: He was giving it away or selling it and I couldn't see anybody hunting damn near full-time just to give it away. It was a mind boggling thought, but the subject helped get my brain back on track a bit.

Mike and I finished our meal, went outside and helped Jimmy finish skinning the elk.

"We can go for a ride up to Weippe this afternoon and maybe find us a moose," Jimmy offered.

"Well," Mike answered. "I promised Donny that my man in Idaho could get us a hundred pounds of moose meat, and I think you're the man, Jimmy."

"If we don't get one tonight, I'm pretty sure we can get one in the morning," Jimmy answered.

Mike and I badly needed to go off somewhere and talk about what we should do, but it wasn't possible. Either Jimmy trusted us to a point, or he had some grand scheme to take us out and kill us on this so-called hunt. There was no question we had Lubinski caught in our web. We had Charbonneau with a deer killed while using artificial light and we had this morning's killing with non-tribal members, but the combined charges would not put him out of business. It was clear that he was having a serious effect on the local populations. Thirty pregnant elk meant sixty elk that were not going to be in the hills come summer. Plus I wasn't sure if this morning's crime scene had been on or off the reservation, we might not even have any jurisdiction on it. One thing I knew, continuing the case wasn't worth getting killed over.

When we were done skinning the elk, I grabbed my daypack out from behind Mike's seat and took it up to our room and closed the door. I pulled my loaded .38 revolver out of its hidey-hole along with a five-shot speed-loader. I had outfitted the gun with Barami grips that had a belt hook and allowed concealment inside my pants with just the very top of the grip showing. I loosened my belt a notch and stuck the gun in my pants above my crotch. I had been wearing my shirttail untucked to fit in with our two crooks and was confident the gun couldn't be seen. And although uncomfortable, it would be fairly accessible both inside and outside the truck. There was no way I could pocket the speed-loader and have any hope to access it if the shit hit the fan so I dumped the five rounds out of it and slipped them in my pants pocket. At least I had ten rounds, five in the gun's cylinder and five somewhat accessible for a reload. All were Federal Hyrda-Shok +P, 129 grain rounds that were as wicked as you could get for the little .38 Special. I was wearing a black ball cap with an NRA logo on it (facing backwards) and if the gun were ever discovered, I was planning on spouting some Second Amendment "you can take my gun from my cold-dead-hand" rhetoric.

I went back outside, looked over at Mike and Jimmy sitting on a couple of old lawn chairs and said, "Let's go get Donny a moose."

Jimmy pulled his .243 out of the truck and loaded two fresh rounds in its magazine. When he closed the bolt, I could not see whether he'd chambered a round or left it empty. I got back in the middle of the bench-seat, and Jimmy snuggled in next to me holding his rifle straight up with his left hand.

As we drove out of Lubinski's driveway, Mike asked, "Which way Jimmy?"

"Head down through 'Fino and get on the highway towards Kamiah, we'll stop and see if my nephew wants to go with us," Jimmy replied.

Another player, I thought. *Was this something innocent or was Charbonneau going to try and leave us in the woods?*

Chapter 12

Going to Church

In Orofino, Mike pulled into a convenience store next to the pumps and asked Jimmy whether he needed anything.

"Just some beer."

Mike got out and put the gas nozzle into the tank. He started the pump, and walked into the station. Jimmy and I sat in the truck, the rifle butt down and the barrel pointed upwards. *This has to look strange,* I thought. *A white guy sitting with a great big fat Indian holding a rifle and it's not even close to hunting season.*

"Don't you ever eat anything solid Jimmy?"

"Not while I'm drinking," he replied. "When I quit, I gotta just drink Mountain Dew."

"I work out of Fairbanks in the summer fighting fires. 'Been doing it for years," I explained. "I work with a lot of Indians and Eskimos. They're Athabascan and Yupik, great people but they drink a hot tea that I swear has more damned sugar in it than water. What's up with the sugar?"

"When I quit drinking I get sicker than a fuckin' dog. I feel like I'm gonna die. It helps me get through it."

Mike walked out carrying a case of Budweiser, handed it into Jimmy, and finished gassing up the truck. We left town with Jimmy drinking a fresh beer, crossed the Clearwater, and turned onto Highway 12, heading upstream along the river.

Mike glanced at Jimmy, "If you caught this undercover prick that's buying fish, what would you do?"

"They'd find him floating in the river," Jimmy spat.

On the outskirts of Kamiah, Jimmy pointed out a trailer court and told Mike to pull in.

"That's Tom sitting on those steps over there," he said pointing to an Indian kid sitting in front of a dilapidated trailer.

"Hey, let's go hunting," Jimmy yelled out the window over to him.

The kid walked over with his head down, and I realized he was older than he had appeared, maybe thirty, black hair, round faced and medium build. A young and almost slim Jimmy.

"Dad raped Sheila last night," he said somberly.

Jimmy glanced over at the trailer, paused and then turned back to Tom. "Your girlfriend?"

"Yeah, she's over at her mother's."

"You should come moose hunting with us," Jimmy suggested. "We'll figure how to get even."

I told Jimmy I'd ride in the back with Tom. There really wasn't enough room for the three of us up front anyway.

As I was getting out, I heard Jimmy talking to Mike, "His dad is my older brother Base. His real name is Basil but we've always just called him Base."

Tom and I got in the back. I pulled the tailgate up and lowered the canopy door. I stuck my hand out to him and introduced myself. I got a halfhearted shake in return;

the guy was down. *At least it doesn't look like Jimmy's up to some villainous scheme,* I thought, and after a bit; *what do you talk about to a man that just had his girlfriend raped by his father?*

"How long you been with this Sheila?"

"A couple of years," he answered and looked down.

The cop in me wanted details of the crime. I also wanted to ask whether it had been reported and if it hadn't I wanted to encourage him. But I couldn't act as though I favored law enforcement. So I just sat there and kept my mouth shut. I had no choice but to play Henderson's persona.

We drove through Kamiah and crossed the Clearwater again. Mike slowed down and turned left off the highway, I looked out the window and saw a sign that read Beaverslide Road. We climbed the east side of the canyon turning on switchbacks back and forth that didn't want to quit.

"You lived in Kamiah your whole life?"

"Mostly I've lived in 'Fino."

"You and Jimmy pretty close?"

"Yeah, he's a good dude."

After the country flattened off Mike pulled over and stopped. He and Jimmy started to get out. I looked around wondering if Jimmy were about to kill something and saw he'd left the rifle in the cab.

I opened the canopy and climbed over the tailgate. We were parked next to a creek with a waterfall. Jimmy walked down a couple of yards and was looking into the pool below the falls.

"The steelhead hang up here for a while before they spawn," he explained. "It doesn't look like they're here yet."

"What crick is this, Jimmy?" I asked.

"Lolo."

Jimmy turned to Tom and asked, "Where's Base keeping his eggs?"

"He's got 'em at the church in Ahsahka. They're in that little building where they keep the food out back and do the Bible study."

"How many he got?"

"I think maybe about fifty gallons," Tom answered. "He keeps 'em in milk jugs plus he's got a bunch of smoked steelhead in there too."

"If we can get them, we oughta get fifteen hundred dollars for that much and we'll get even," Jimmy said.

"What kind of eggs are you talking about?" I asked.

"Steelhead, there's a guy up north that buys 'em."

"He sell 'em for bait or what?" Mike asked.

"Yeah, you white guys use 'em," Jimmy scowled.

Charbonneau's response had an edge to it. But I couldn't tell for sure whether it was directed at Mike and me or was rooted by what his diabolical brother had done. Unmistakably, Charbonneau had become bad-tempered and his mood seemed as if it could be focusing on us.

The nightmare-like scene we'd walked into boggled me. A father had raped his son's girlfriend, and now the brother of the rapist was conspiring with the rapist's son, to commit a burglary to get even. Beyond the insanity of what had happened to Tom and his lady, I was mystified by Jimmy and Tom's discussion of getting even. Listening to Jimmy's proposal, it didn't sound as though he was simply fueled by revenge. His unbridled interest in what the eggs were worth was clear—he wanted the money.

We got back in the truck and continued up the gravel road. It was timber country with a few intermixed clear-cuts. When we drove out of the timber and into a cut, Mike would slow down, and I could see Jimmy through the rear window looking hard, but the critters must have been laying low, since we saw none in the midday warmth.

Mike stopped at a creek, got out, and walked behind some brush to pee. Tom and I crawled out of the back. I was glad to get out. Between the corrugated steel and the rough road, it was not a fun place to ride.

Jimmy spoke to Tom. "We'll have to get some bolt cutters and maybe a crowbar."

Mike came over to me and took a seat on a log. I sat down and joined him.

"Jimmy says he used to sell meat to a guy in Montana, and they had code words worked out," Mike said with Jimmy standing nearby.

"What d'ya mean, code words?" I asked. "What are you talking about?"

"A small sack of potatoes were for deer, a sack of red potatoes was elk, and black walnuts meant moose," he explained.

"Oh," I paused. "So you can talk about it and nobody can understand. That's a damn good idea."

Jimmy joined us on the log. "You guys like smoked steelhead?"

"Well, smoked salmon," I answered. "Can't say I've ever had smoked steelhead, Pate and I can't catch 'em."

"Tom and I should get a bunch tonight."

"Well," Mike said. "I know Donny'd be interested if it's good. If it's junk he won't buy it."

We climbed back in the truck and bounced down the road back in the direction we had come from. I was happy when we finally hit the highway. When we crossed the river into Orofino, Mike turned up into an alley and pulled in front of a grungy Quonset hut with a sign proclaiming chainsaw repair. Jimmy got out of the passenger seat and walked into the place. He came out after a couple of minutes, walked back to the rear of the truck, cracked the canopy door open, and looked at Tom shaking his head. "Bob won't loan us a bolt cutter, maybe Rex's got one."

We headed back for the Crabtree. Mike stopped at Snow's Rock, and we all got out and let it rain. At the lodge, we found Rex drinking beer in the dining room with Carol. Robert was smoking a cigarette in the living room and chatting with Trudy and Adrian.

"Yous guys find a moose?" Rex asked.

"No, but we need to borrow some tools," Jimmy stated.

Rex sensed something was afoot. He got up and engaged Jimmy on the other side of the room. I could see Rex nodding and could hear enough to tell that Jimmy was talking about stealing his brother's eggs. The two disappeared into the garage. Jimmy came out with a set of bolt cutters and a crow bar, laid the tools by the door, and sat down on the couch with a beer next to the two kids.

Rex returned to the table and told Robert to start dinner. Robert didn't comment, stood up and lit another cigarette as he walked into the kitchen. I didn't bother to look to see whether he would wash his hands.

I was just flat-out pooped and told Rex I would lie down for a bit and asked him to holler when dinner was ready. In the room, I pulled the .38 out of my pants and stuck it back in the hidden pocket of my daypack. It had not been a comfortable "carry" inside my pants while I'd bounced around the back of the truck and was glad to put it away. But nonetheless it could have been fatally stupid not to have it handy. I heard Mike's familiar gait as he came into the room. We both laid down on our beds and neither of us said a word. I was still shaken-up about what Jimmy had told us about the undercover sting, and I needed to talk about it to Mike but it wouldn't happen inside the Crabtree.

I lay there and thought about our situation. If Jimmy were suspicious about us, I surely wouldn't think he'd be openly planning a burglary in front of us. What I *was sure about* was that we couldn't do anything that would focus the slightest suspicion on us. My thoughts shifted to the planned burglary and how to deal with it. There really wasn't anyway to drop a dime on what the two were planning and I couldn't see anyway to prevent it. If they wanted to commit a felony then so be it as long as it didn't include violence, we would just sit back and document the details of the crime for a later prosecution.

"Hey, dinner's ready," Rex yelled up.

I stood up and whispered to Mike, "I wonder what church they'll hit?"

"Jimmy pointed it out to me, it's that little white one next to the hatchery," he whispered back.

We walked down stairs. Jimmy was sipping beer and talking to Trudy in the living room. Tom and Rex were sitting at the dining table. Mike and I sat down and joined them. Robert and Carol had disappeared, and I assumed they had gone to their room. The meal was the standard wild game and potatoes that had become infamous.

"What kinda meat's this?" I asked.

"It's the tenderloins from the elk you guys got this morning," Rex said.

The meat was tough and had an uncharacteristic gamey taste for elk. I blamed the flavor on the time of year. Elk and deer were at their absolute worst physical condition going into green-up. Nonetheless, I wolfed it down; it had been a long time since brunch.

I sat there at the table thinking about Lubinski and his operation. The lodge was rather pleasant but dirty. We'd never seen any guests other than ourselves. Robert was supposedly his manager but there wasn't much to manage. Rex was obviously using Jimmy for a source of cheap meat. And there was the fact that we'd gone out with Jimmy that morning, killed an elk that supposedly Donny was buying for his game feed from Jimmy, and Rex had removed the choicest cuts and no-doubt would charge *us* for the meal. Sleazy to say the least.

Lubinski's lifestyle got me thinking about Jimmy's. I knew he owned a leaky camp trailer that sat on blocks, a rifle, fishing pole, rope, axe, and a knife and that was probably about it. He had no truck, or a car, no phone, and it looked as though he had no legitimate income. It appeared that during the spring steelhead run he spent most days snagging fish in front of the hatchery. His trailer was a mile or two from the hatchery, and Jimmy surely wasn't walking back and forth. He was "harvesting" hundreds of fish a year and somehow moving them in commerce without a rig or a phone plus he was apparently killing twenty or thirty elk a year. If it weren't for the rumors of an undercover sting. I would have tried to get him to talk about his lifestyle but this was no time to be nosey.

I looked over where he had been sitting, and Jimmy was gone. I glanced around and saw Robert and Carol sitting with Rex but no Tom. I walked upstairs to the room and found Mike, he had just gotten out of the shower and I told him that Jimmy and Tom had apparently disappeared.

"Well," Mike whispered. "I heard the Gremlin start up a minute ago. Maybe they're gonna hit the church."

"That's curious," I answered. "Rex is down stairs drinking with Robert and Carol. I wonder who is driving, Jimmy sure as hell doesn't have a license and Tom probably doesn't either."

Lubinski knew he was providing tools for a burglary and his support was *felony aid-and-abet*; it was a great charge to add to his list but we'd need to shore it up with an admission from him. I went back down and helped myself to a Keystone thinking it was time to blend in and wait for the two thieves to return.

"Rex, where'd Jimmy and Tom go?"

"They's out taking care of business," he said with a knowing grin.

I looked out past the hot tub. "Looks like it's raining," I said. I walked over to the sliding glass door and stepped outside. A steady drizzle was coming down. I looked past the yard light and beyond it was as dark as a black dog. I stepped out into the night, walked past the lamp, and into the darkness. I stood there taking a pee smelling the dampness of the spring night. It was good to get out of the fouled odor of the lodge. I dumped most of the Keystone in the gravel and walked back inside. I sat down with Rex and picked up an Outdoor Life and thumbed through it glancing at its inane stories. It was time to settle in and see what the night brought.

Mike and I had been up for about fifteen hours, I could see a light coming from our room's doorway but couldn't hear Mike moving. He was either reading or had fallen asleep. I heard the rumble of the Gremlin pull in outside, and then Jimmy and Tom came in. As much as I had been around Jimmy with his constant beer drinking he had never *looked or sounded drunk*. But, now both of the Charbonneaus had the uncoordinated lurch of drunkenness.

"We gotta make another run; the car wouldn't hold it all," Jimmy slurred.

He stumbled back out the door with Tom mimicking his drunken dance. Rex followed, and I tagged along. The Gremlin was piled with pinkish frozen milk jugs, bags of smoked fish and several loose frozen steelhead. I helped the three unload the stash into Rex's garage next to the unskinned Swamp Creek deer.

"My sister got arrested," Jimmy said. "You got any bail money I can have Rex?"

"I think I got sixty bucks," Rex scowled. He pulled three twenties out of his chain-wallet, and handed the money to Jimmy.

Jimmy turned to Tom and slurred, "Let's go get your aunt out'a jail and then we'll get the rest of the eggs."

"Jimmy," I said. "You're gonna get your ass arrested, you're too goddamned drunk. I'll drive." There was no way I could allow them to be on the road, and the only thing I could think of was to jump into the core of it. Besides, they were in the middle of a felony and I needed more information to ensure their prosecution. I opened the driver's door, sat down on the springy seat, and found the key in the ignition and twisted it. The noisy little beast growled to life. There was no sense searching for my seat belt; the floor of the Gremlin was carpeted with smashed beer cans. Tom got in the back seat, and big Jimmy slid his drunken ass in beside me. Neither of them said a word as I dropped down the grade.

"Where we heading, Jimmy?" I asked.

"Take us down to the jail, I have to bail my sister out first."

I could smell whiskey on his breath, and it explained why he was so drunk. I really doubted that he could have gotten this drunk on beer alone.

"What'd she get arrested for?" I asked.

"DUI," Jimmy answered.

We drove on down past Snow's Rock, the headlights were a dull yellow and didn't light much up with the rain drizzling in the darkness. I got to the bottom of the hill, crossed the North Fork and drove past the hatchery. The rain picked up its pace.

"Where the hell's the wiper switch?" I asked.

"They don't work," Jimmy drawled.

"You're gonna have to help me out, where the hell's the jail?" I lied.

He directed me up Michigan Street which was really Main Street.

"Drop me off at the Jet Club, first eh?" Tom asked.

I swung a block over and turned right. My driver's door suddenly swung open, and I leaned out and grabbed the damned thing while trying to hang on and steer simultaneously.

"You gotta hold it closed when you turn right, it don't shut," Jimmy blurted.

I pulled in front of the Jet Club and stopped. Jimmy struggled out, and Tom emerged from behind him.

"Come get me when you get her out," Tom said.

Jimmy crawled back in and resumed his seat. I drove around the block holding the driver's door closed.

"Just pull up in there, that's the jail," Jimmy said pointing.

"I'll stay here with the rig." For all I knew there was a deputy working the jail that I had gone to the police academy with, and it was the last place I wanted to be right now.

After a few minutes, the door opened and Jimmy came staggering out. I saw a uniform watching him from a window as he shuffle down the steps and climbed into the passenger side of the Gremlin.

"She already bonded out," he explained.

I turned the yellow headlights on and headed back to the Jet Club and found a place to park. I tried to take the key out of the ignition, but it was stuck, and I got out thinking, *who would want to steal this piece of crap anyway?*

Jimmy and I walked into the stench of the Jet Club. Stratified smoke filled the place, I looked around and the same caricatures were sitting in the same places from my last visit or at least their clones. The bartender with the weird eyes looked up at Jimmy and went back to pouring a drink. I spotted Tom sitting at a table in the rear with two brunettes in their late twenties. Jimmy and I walked back and joined them. It was obvious everybody knew Jimmy and accepted me without inquiry. The waitress was standing talking to Tom and the two females. The two could have passed for sisters, and maybe they were. The waitress asked what I wanted, and I told her a bottle of Budweiser. Jimmy ordered a Jack Daniels, and she left for the bar. I got a better look at the two women— they were mixed blood, Nez Perce and white. Both were raw and uninhibitedly attractive.

The taller of the two women was smoking and talking to Tom. "I've been raped twice." She sounded like a divorcee talking about her bad marriages. It was clear she was trying to console him.

The cocktail waitress brought our drinks, I gave her a twenty and she laid my change down on the table. I took a drink of Bud and looked at Jimmy; he'd drunk half his whiskey in one big slurp while I was paying for the drinks.

He looked back at me and said, "You're DWI now," and laughed at himself. He went on an explained his joke. "DWI, that's Drinking-With-Indians," and snickered again.

I smiled back at him, stood up and walked into the men's room carrying my beer. A drunk left the urinal, I stepped up to it and dumped most of my beer into it. I thought about Jimmy Charbonneau's mood. He was enjoying his drunkenness but I wasn't convinced he was enjoying my company.

I walked back through the bar and sat back down at the table. The closest gal met my eyes and inhaled her cigarette without breaking her gaze. After a pause she pursed her lips, softly exhaled her smoke, and gave me a mischievous smile. I twinkled back, took a swallow of Bud and turned to Jimmy, "Don't we need to get some stuff tonight?"

"Tom," Jimmy slurred. "We need to get our asses moving."

I finished the two inches of my beer, nodded at the temptress still looking at me, left a tip for the waitress, and stood up. Jimmy's drink was dry, and Tom swallowed what was left of his and crunched an ice cube. The three of us walked out to the street. Nobody had stolen Rex's Gremlin.

I opened the door, stepped in on the smashed cans and sat down. The engine started up, Jimmy and Tom took their seats and I caught a whiff of urine.

"Where to, Jimmy?"

"Go back down by the hatchery."

I crossed Michigan Street and turned right on Riverside remembering to hold my door shut. Just before the hatchery Jimmy said, "Pull in there and cut your lights off."

I stopped in front of a closed chain-link gate topped with barbed wire. There was a cut lock dangling from its heavy chain that stuck out like a lone tree in a park. I killed the lights. *It really was showtime.*

Jimmy took a pair of leather gloves off the cracked dash, and walked over to the gate. He swung one side open, and I drove into the church grounds leaving enough room for Jimmy to close the gate. He got back in, and I crept the car ahead. It was too dark and rainy to see the road without the lights through the wet windshield, but I could see the ghost of the white church for a reference. I rolled down the window and stuck my head out into the rain and eased the car forward.

"Pull in just next to the church by the other building," Jimmy ordered.

I eased over to it, shut the car down and stepped out into the darkness. I could see headlights coming from Orofino. Jimmy and Tom noticed too and we froze.

"If it's a cop, run for the goddamned river, they don't like me," Jimmy said ominously.

I held my breath as the vehicle slowed near the gate but continued on towards the hatchery. It was too dark to see anything but its head and tail lights. *Had they seen the hanging lock or maybe some reflection off the Gremlin?*

I'd felt oddly at ease in the Jet Club and driving Rex's junker around town, but this situation was a different deal. I was right smack in the middle of a felony. If a deputy saw the cut lock hanging on the gate, and a good one would be looking, he'd have to check it out. He'd probably choose a tactical approach on foot through the timber from the hatchery or some other angle. No doubt, he'd bring his short-barreled shotgun loaded with double-aught buckshot. It would be an easy approach to make after his eyes adjusted to the darkness, the drizzle would cover his noise. He'd find the three of us loading the car, raise his shotgun, and yell out, "Sheriff! Don't move!" If Jimmy or Tom made a furtive gesture, the deputy might pull the trigger and eight .33 caliber lead balls would scream out of his barrel. It was a stupid place for me to be.

Jimmy and Tom had gone through the open door of the building next to the church. I walked in behind them, and Jimmy turned a flashlight on. There were hymnbooks stacked on a bookcase and six open Bibles lay on a table as if we'd interrupted Bible class. Two chest freezers were along the opposite wall. I heard another vehicle and Jimmy shut the light off. We held our breath and listened as it drove on by. The flashlight came back on.

"Let's get this shit loaded," Tom said.

The demeanor of the two Indians was queer. They were both drunker than skunks and dead sober at the same time. Focused on the moment. Both were fumbling for muscle control and it was reflected by their heavily slurred speech. But, they seemed acutely cognitive and I believed they were cranked on the trepidation of what was afoot.

Jimmy opened one of the freezer lids with his gloved hands. Several plastic milk jugs tinted pink by fish eggs lay in the freezer. Tom reached in and grabbed an armload of containers with his gloved-up hands. I followed Tom out with four cold jugs in my arms and loaded them in the back of the Gremlin. I looked into the night and couldn't see the nearby church, Jimmy's light had night-blinded me.

We got the twenty or so egg jugs loaded in the car. We jumped back into the Gremlin and drove to the gate with the lights off. Jimmy opened it and I drove us through. He left the gate open and jumped back in.

"Let's get the fuck out of here," Jimmy said.

It was the best idea I'd heard all week. I hit the lights, turned left onto the road and drove past the hatchery. We crossed the North Fork and turned right coming off the bridge. My door swung fully open with the momentum, and I burst out laughing going by the Woodlot. The night had been ludicrous, an insane on-the-job escapade.

I turned up the grade and had the urge to urinate as we passed Snow's Rock, but I continued up to Lube's lodge. I backed the noisy beast to the garage. The light came on inside, and I saw Rex raising the door. I shut the Gremlin off and got out.

"Hey," Mike said out of nowhere from the darkness. "Where you been, buddy? You just up and disappeared."

"Well," I paused... "I had to go to church."

Chapter 13

The Heat is On

The next morning things were quiet at the Crabtree. The previous day had taken its toll. Jimmy and Tom were drinking beer, *the hair of the dog*, in an apparent effort to medicate their hangovers. I was ragged, and Mike looked the same. The fatigue wasn't simply the physical activity; the early morning so-called hunt, the Beaverslide drive, or the church burglary. It was the cumulative physical effort plus the added weightiness of undercover—the constant paranoiac endeavor of maintaining cover; never forgetting the role that needed played; outlaw Tony Henderson. It was the struggle between my emotional and cognitive processes. I felt as if I had been in a continual "fight or flight" state while holding my cards tight. I wished I could just click my heels three times and be back home with my dog, Ben.

Robert had cooked eggs and hash browns and had left them wrapped in foil in the oven. Mike and I helped ourselves and sat down with food and coffee. Jimmy picked up Lubinski's phone and made a call.

"Hey, what's Shawn's number?"

I watched him write down something on a piece of paper and hang up. He made a second call. "Shawn, this is Jimmy in 'Fino," he paused, "I ripped my brother's eggs off last night and got about thirty gallons. How much you paying?" He listened for a moment, grunted and hung up. He took a long pull from his beer, finishing it and burped. He turned to Tom. "We're gonna get about five-hundred for the eggs."

Neither showed any disappointment (or enthusiasm) over the diminished value of Base's eggs, even though it was much less than the anticipated $1500. Both seemed indifferent about the rape and the burglary, they were closemouthed and emotionless, maybe it was the hangover, or maybe they were just keeping it in. I was still confused on whether it was greed or revenge that had motivated the theft, and I couldn't quite swallow that Tom believed retribution had been discharged. What clarity I grasped was that I was dancing with a culture that I didn't understand.

I sipped my coffee and thought about the fish eggs taken from the church. I guessed it would take about five female steelhead to fill a gallon jug with eggs, maybe less, but multiplying the figure by thirty jugs gave me an estimated number of females. Doubling the number to include males, I figured Basil Charbonneau had caught about three hundred steelhead to fill the thirty containers. The two Charbonneau boys had apparently caught roughly 600 steelhead this winter. They had to be selling most of them. Jimmy had said he traded fish for marijuana and Snow had heard the same rumor about he and a guy up at Avery.

"Hey, Jimmy," I said. "Did Base catch all those fish at the hatchery or does he have some secret hole where Pate and I could maybe catch one without getting our asses thrown in jail?"

"Yeah, he just fishes at the hatchery, I taught him everything he knows," Jimmy said. "You might try down by the Pole Yard."

"Where's that?" I asked.

"It's kinda across from the hatchery right there where the North Fork comes in; I think there should be some fish hanging there."

It sounded like Basil Charbonneau had caught the fish himself and wasn't just buying eggs at wholesale. If he had been buying from other Indians, Jimmy hadn't brought it up.

I heard Lube in the background on the phone, "Earl, this is Rex at the Crabtree. Hey, I've got a bunch of smoked steelhead up here I'm selling real cheap. Come on up if you want some."

Twenty minutes later an older male walked in and handed Rex what looked like a couple of twenty-dollar bills.

"Do you guys need some help loading some of that stuff?" I asked the two.

"Yeah," Rex answered. "If you wouldn't mind."

I went back to the garage, opened up the overhead door and met the older guy. "You buy one or two sacks? I'm Tony by the way, what's your name?"

"It's Earl, I paid for two."

I helped him with the load and noted his license plate. *Sale of steelhead,* I thought.

I went back in and helped myself to another cup of coffee.

Mike spoke up. "Let's all go on down to the Woodlot and have one of their fine burgers, I'm buying."

The five of us walked out. Rex, Jimmy, and Tom got in the Gremlin and drove out the driveway. Mike and I got in our rig and headed down behind them. Mike looked over at me, frowned and shook his head. "That was one crazy night."

"No," I answered. "It wasn't crazy, it was insane. You need to put me in the nut house when we get back; I could use the rest. And by the way, on the way outa this hole, we need to talk about that undercover thing Jimmy told us about."

"You know it, buddy," Mike nodded.

We pulled into the Woodlot and parked next to Rex's green machine and walked in.

Rex, Jimmy, and Tom were sitting with an unknown couple. He was in his late thirties, wearing wire-rimmed glasses, had curly hair, and a matching three-day beard. She was attractive with long dark hair and was probably in her late twenties. Both were smoking and drinking draft beer.

"This is Mickey White and Judy," Rex said, "They live in Avery and come down here quite a bit."

Mickey White stuck his hand out to me. "I wanna shake your hand, you look just like Claude Dallas, and he's my hero."

I reached over and shook his hand, but I doubt it was with much conviction. On top of the realization, that this was the drug dealer who was swapping marijuana for steelhead. His comment about worshipping a game warden killer had staggered me. I wasn't prepared for it.

Mike sensed my uneasiness and took him off guard. "You guys down here fishing or honeymooning?"

Mickey laughed and shook Mike's hand. "Fishing and partying, aren't we, babe?" he said and turned to Judy.

"Yeah, and getting some fish from Jimmy," she added. "Last year I snagged with him at the hatchery. I claimed I was his wife; it was a blast."

"You catch any lately?" I asked.

"No, we just got in, but we're gonna fish the Pole Yard in a while."

"Jimmy said that was a good place, I need to try that hole sometime."

"Well if you see us down there, I'll show you how to fish it," Mickey offered.

We ate our burgers, and Mike and I drank coffee in lieu of the beer that everybody else was drinking. During the meal, plans were made to hunt moose in the afternoon with Jimmy. *Greedy bastards,* I thought. The Swamp Creek deer was still hanging in Lube's garage, and Charbonneau had killed the elk that Rex would process and ship half of it down to "Donny." Between the deer and half the elk, Lube had plenty of (illegal) meat. And there was the grouse he had killed that had been forgotten under the seat in Mike's truck.

Rex said he'd be back up to the lodge sometime later and to hang out for a while. We got back in the truck and headed up the grade.

Well," I said. "We met Mickey. You got any ideas on what we can do with him? He's definitely a player."

"Let's just cogitate on it. 'Seems we've got enough going right now, but maybe we can get a chance to fish with him or something."

Just what I wanted to do, I thought, *fish with Claude Dallas's number one fan.*

We drove back up to the lodge, hoping to get a private moment to photograph Lube's eagle feather, but Trudy and Adrian were hanging out in the living room together. Robert's car was gone, and there was no sign of Carol. I lay down on my bed and woke up to the noise of the Gremlin. I threw my shoes on and went down to see what the plan was.

Rex and Jimmy were in the living room talking to the kids. Jimmy was staggering drunk. Rex looked over at us, and I could tell he was frustrated by Jimmy's state. It was obvious the planned hunt was off.

Mike told Rex that we needed to get some gas. We got back in Mike's rig and headed to 'Fino. It was only day four, and I was tired of this so-called adventure. The fatigue was wearing on Mike too. He suggested we go down by the river and chill out for a while. We drove down the grade and crossed the North Fork. Mike wanted to see where the theft had taken place, and we turned into the church's driveway. The gate was open, but I noticed it was sporting a larger lock and chain. We drove in, and Mike pointed at a sign; "Ahsahka Nez Perce Presbyterian Church, built in 1890."

"That's amazing," Mike exclaimed. "That's probably where Chief Joseph went to church. And you, Henderson. You robbed it. You're going to Hell for sure," he looked over at me laughing.

"I think I'm clean on that one, I don't believe the government ever let Joseph back here after the war."

We drove past the church and parked near the river. It was warm and sunny, a good time to be away from the cigarette smell of the Crabtree.

We walked along the river. The spring warming had caused the river to raise a bit and color up with mud.

Mike stooped over and picked up a small rock. "Hey, looky here buddy, an arrowhead."

It was made from obsidian and about an inch and a half long with a tiny portion of the tip broken off. The point's maker had chipped notches into the upper corners to lash to its shaft.

"Pate," I said. "That thing's older than you are."

"Yeah, probably by a few thousand years."

We sat down and marveled at the piece. Mike was right, an Indian had made it centuries ago, maybe even thousands. I looked hard at the parallel flakes coming off the edges. The erosion of years had taken its sharpness. It was a manifestation of how the people and the country had been changed at Ahsahka.

Getting away from the Crabtree and its soul revitalized Mike and me, but we were annoyed by Charbonneau's drunken unreliability; we were wasting time. We drove over to the phone booth near the Woodlot and tried to call Snow and got his machine. Mike left a short message and dialed a second number. It was obviously ringing and ringing.

"Who you calling now?" I asked.

"My boss. I thought I'd call the office and let Roger know we're still alive."

"Yeah, well it's Saturday and the rest of the world doesn't work on the weekend."

Mike laughed and hung the phone up. We got back in his truck and headed up the grade for the Crabtree. Just before we got to Snow's Rock we met Rex coming down. Jimmy was sitting in the passenger seat with his eyes anchored forward. Rex slowed to a stop and rolled his window down.

"I'm taking Jimmy down to drop him off; I might be late getting back," Rex explained.

Obviously he was pissed with the big Indian. We continued up the hill and when we hit the driveway leading into the lodge Mike stopped and turned to me. "Let's just go to town and get a good dinner by ourselves, I ain't ready for this place yet."

I agreed. We turned around and headed for Orofino. Just past the hatchery we came around a corner and had to quickly decelerate to avoid hitting the rear of a Clearwater County sheriff's SUV. The rig's light bar was lit up in a flashing blue manic display. It was stopped in our lane with both doors open. An officer on the passenger side had a shotgun thrust through his open window pointing towards the car that was in front of their rig. A second officer had his pistol out and pointed out the driver's side window. I glanced at the car they had stopped; it was the Gremlin. There were two suspects face down on the ground between the two vehicles, the unmistakable outlines of Jimmy Charbonneau and Rex Lubinski lying prone with arms straight out.

Mike looked at me, rolled his eyes and drove around the arrest scene.

"Its got to be the burglary," I said, shaking my head.

"Yeah, but how did they put it together?"

"Shit," I said shaking my head. "Jimmy told the egg buyer. Maybe he dropped a dime. These numbskulls are flapping their jowls. Who knows, maybe it was that Earl guy?"

"Well," Mike paused. "If it's the burglary we might have to take this case down, but shit, I want to get into the buyers."

"Yeah," I added. "If it's the burglary it's game over." There was no way we could stay undercover while a prosecution commenced on one of crimes we had knowledge of and if we had to start the prosecution of one count, we'd have to start them all. It would involve serving search warrants, making arrests, and interviewing both the perps and any potential witnesses such as Robert. It would take a lot of planning and paper work and the prosecutor had no knowledge of the case. It would be a bad way to start a prosecution.

"Let's call up to the lodge and see whether Robert's back and maybe he knows something," I suggested.

We found a pay phone at the Texaco station. I put some quarters in and dialed the Crabtree. On the third ring, Adrian answered.

"Hey, this is Tony. Can I speak with Robert?"

"No, he's not here," he said whimpering.

"What's going on?"

"Jimmy raped Trudy," he sobbed.

Again I was stunned, but this time it was worse. A little kid, raped by a three hundred and thirty-pound drunken slob. I mumbled something and hung up, turned to Mike and told him what I'd just heard. We just stood there for a moment looking at each other.

"Jimmy's a sociopath," Mike said after a bit.

We decided to eat at the Ponderosa. Although it was Saturday, the place had few patrons and we had plenty of room to talk, but neither one of us had much to say. The food was unremarkable, but it wasn't the cook's fault. I thought about the Charbonneau brothers and the arrowhead with its dulled edges. I also thought about Jimmy's reaction to his brother raping his son's girlfriend and decided it wasn't the revenge that motivated the theft; it was raw greed. The rape had just been an excuse. Mike was right; Jimmy Charbonneau was a sociopath.

We talked about what might happen as the result of the recent development and decided there was a good chance a search warrant would be executed at the Crabtree. Although Lubinski's lodge was private property, it was within the borders of the Nez Perce Indian Reservation; therefore, since Charbonneau was a tribal member the case fell under the FBI's umbrella. The back of our truck still had blood in it from the elk and the deer we'd hauled plus plenty of tale-tell ungulate hair that wouldn't lie. If the rape investigators saw the blood, they might impound our truck or at least get Snow involved. The simplest solution to this potential challenge would be to clean it out. After we finished dinner we drove to a car wash up Michigan Street and washed the blood and hair from the bed and tailgate. I felt like a crook destroying evidence.

As we pulled out of the bay, Mike saw Tom Charbonneau in the parking lot across the street and drove over to him and rolled his window down and stuck his head out.

"Tom," Mike said. "I think Jimmy got arrested for rape."

"Who'd he rape?"

"That little girl up at the lodge, Trudy."

Tom's only response was a slight widening of his eyes, and then he glanced away looking back at the car wash.

"We were goin' moose hunting with him tomorrow too," Mike added.

Tom's head swiveled around like a tank turret. "Just take me instead."

"That would be great, man," Mike responded.

"Pick me up at my trailer at six then," Tom added. "You guys want to buy any of that smoked fish we took from the church?"

"Let me call Donny and ask him whether he's interested," Mike answered. "How much you want a bag?"

"Fifteen."

"How 'bout I tell him twelve bucks a bag?"

"Sure, I'll see you at six tomorrow at my trailer."

We'd just scooped Tom up. We had him wrapped around the burglary but didn't have any knowledge of his trafficking. Unequivocally, he was more than willing to follow in his uncle's (and probably his father's) footsteps, at least with wildlife. Besides, he wanted to sell us evidence of the burglary. There was no judicial reason for us to turn him down on his offers. But, I was disappointed he'd just stuck his greedy foot in our trap. I liked the kid, and felt sorry for him. I knew why. I'd just contracted a touch of Stockholm Syndrome and would have to deal with it.

When we returned to the Crabtree, Robert's K-car was gone but both of Rex's rigs were there. Robert and Carol had probably left the Crabtree for good.

Rex was sour when we walked in the door. He claimed he didn't know anything and was blaming Trudy or her mother for whatever might have happened. He didn't seem worried about his so-called friend Jimmy Charbonneau; he was worried about himself.

"The heat is on," Rex blurted. "The cops are gonna be up here for sure, maybe the Fish and Game."

He had pulled a domestic ram skull and horns out of the garage and told us they were from a bighorn sheep. Internally, Mike and I were both doing eye rolls over his misidentification and concern over nothing.

"I'm gonna hide these and the elk antlers out back. I think the deer and the elk we got hanging is okay 'cause I'm just going to tell them that Jimmy has been staying up here, and they're his. They can't do nothing about that. But, if you get a moose tomorrow with Tom, take it to his place and not back here. Believe me, the heat is on."

I looked Lube in the eye, "You and I need to have a heart-to-heart." And marched him into our room and closed the door carrying a pissed-off contrived attitude.

We stood face-to-face three feet apart. "You need to understand something," I said staring into his eyes.

"You'd better not take Pate down on this. He's worth a lot of money, and he's been real good to me and it's going to stay that goddamned way. I don't care if I have to do some jail time, but we are not going to get Pate's ass thrown in jail. It ain't gonna happen," I went on with my voice getting lower and my eyes tighter. "Things are too fucking loose here; Mickey White knows what's going on; Robert Deacon knows what's going on. You're running a leaky fucking ship here, and this boat is gonna sink if you don't keep your fucking mouth shut, you understand?"

Rex's eye's had gotten bigger as I'd chewed him out. I wanted him to believe that money was in the air and I too was a greedy crooked bastard. It seemed to have the desired effect.

"You don't have to worry about Mickey, he's a big drug dealer and brings a lot of dope in. I'll make sure Robert keeps his mouth shut—he owes me big time," Rex continued. "And Jimmy told me about his old code words, a small sack of potatoes is deer and black walnuts is moose; I'll start using 'em on receipts and stuff."

I stood there and stared at him for a few seconds cooling off and letting it soak into his skin. My rendition had left me with a satisfied feeling. It was good to yell at Lubinski. And for a few minutes Tony Henderson was real.

Chapter 14

Lewd & Lascivious

The next morning Mike and I left the Crabtree at 5:30 a.m. with cups of coffee and empty stomachs. We crossed the Clearwater and headed upriver to Kamiah.

It didn't look as if anybody were awake at Tom's trailer when we got there. Mike knocked on the door and after a couple of minutes I could hear somebody moving inside. A woman answered the door who had obviously just gotten out of bed; she was in her late twenties and Nez Perce. I assumed she was Sheila, Tom's girlfriend, but I didn't ask. She told us that she didn't know where Tom was. However, she'd heard he was going hunting and directed us to another trailer in a different park in Kamiah. We found the trailer easily enough, but nobody answered the door.

What to do? We drove around and finally found a cafe that was open; at least we could fill our bellies. After the meal, we hit the trailer courts again and couldn't find Tom. We were back on Indian Time and headed for Ahsahka.

As we passed the Woodlot, I noticed the Gremlin, and Mike pulled in. Mickey and Judy were sitting at a table drinking coffee and smoking. Rex was sitting with them, but he was drinking the "breakfast of champions" even though it was just south of 10:00 a.m. We sat down with the threesome and told them about our woes with our

AWOL friend. They all smiled knowingly about the unreliability of the Charbonneau clan.

"I think Jimmy's getting outa jail this afternoon," Rex volunteered. "I want to go check out an auction inventory down at Lapwai, and then I'll go see whether Jimmy's out and what he wants to do."

Mickey turned to me. "We're gonna fish the Pole Yard in a minute; you wanna go?"

"Yeah," I answered. "Maybe the steelhead gods will finally smile on me."

Mike spoke to Rex. "I'll check out the auction place with you, if you don't mind."

I pulled my fishing rod out from behind Mike's seat and jumped in the back of Mickey's car. It was an older maroon Ford Crown Vic, the same model that was such a hit with city cops. It wasn't the "Police Interceptor" version, but it was equipped with an odor: The pungent smell of burnt weed.

We drove past the North Fork Bridge, turned off the Ahsahka Grade, and parked behind a log deck. The main Clearwater was still running color from spring run off. The Pole Yard Hole was just below the confluence of the North Fork, and was fed by clear water. Since it was the first holding water below the hatchery, it looked promising. Although I wanted to catch a steelhead, I didn't want to fish with this idolizer of Claude Dallas, but it was time to get to work and gain some information that would hopefully lead somewhere.

Mickey pointed at the run. "They lay in the North Fork just along the main's mud-line. Cast out into the Clearwater and let it drift into this clear stuff." He mentioned the fact that he'd never seen a game warden at this hole. He opened up his tackle box and showed me how he rigged for steelhead. As I expected, he didn't pinch the hook's barb down as required by the regulations. I rigged up mimicking his method. Judy seemed like a nice woman, much too fine for this game warden-loathing drug dealer. I wondered if I weren't coming down with another bout of Stockholm Syndrome.

After a few casts through the hole, Mickey rolled a joint, lit it up, and handed it to Judy. She took a deep hit, held it in, and then handed it to me; maybe she was the perfect match for Mickey after all.

"No thanks. I gotta start work in a couple of weeks and I'll have to take a pee-test."

Mickey took the roach, sucked more of the smoke into his system and held it. He exhaled and looked at Judy. "I wonder if there's some new dope in town yet? This stuff is rank. We oughta know by nine."

His comment told me he'd probably swallowed my excuse.

"I fish for pike up at Black Lake above Avery," Mickey said and took another hit. He held it a bit and then let it out as he spoke. "There's a cabin we use there. I been putting a set line out at night, but I ain't got it perfected yet."

"What do you mean, a set line?"

"I tie on about ten feet of line to a small milk jug with a great big four-ought hook on it. Then I catch up a little bass or perch 'bout six inches long or so, and put the hook through its back and let it swim around dragging the jug all night. So far I've only lost one rig."

"You get any that way?"

"Yeah, I got a twenty-eight incher last time we was up there."

After the marijuana, Mickey retrieved a cooler from his Ford and handed me a Keystone. It was still pre-noon, but I felt it would be stupid to pass. We fished, drank beer, and small talked. I brought up Jimmy Charbonneau's woes, hoping it would get him talking about steelhead dope-deals.

"This isn't the first time Jimmy's done that," Mickey said.

"You mean with some kid?" I asked.

"Yeah, I don't know how old the other one was."

I didn't ask for further details. My comment about Jimmy hadn't brought out the desired information. Whatever sexual crimes Jimmy had committed earlier weren't going to get charged if they hadn't surfaced by now. After two hours of casting and talking about nothing, I heard Mike holler from behind us. "Hey, Henderson, you catch a steelhead yet?"

I turned and answered, "Hell no, you ready to go eat something?"

"Yeah, you betcha, 'cause Jimmy's out and we gotta see whether we can get us a moose this evening."

It was good news, I wasn't enthusiastic about road hunting with Jimmy the sociopath or watching something else die. But I was tired of putting up with Mickey White's jabber.

I thanked the two dopers and got in with Mike. I briefed him on what I had learned, which wasn't much. Mike explained that Rex had picked Jimmy up at the jail, and according to Rex, he'd asked whether we still wanted to go moose hunting in the evening. He was fresh out of jail and eager to break the law with us—a true recidivist.

We picked up a couple of burgers at the Woodlot and headed back to the lodge. It was a warm sunny day, and Mike and I decided to eat outside. I was about halfway into my burger when a dark SUV pulled up to the lodge. A guy stepped out wearing a sport coat and he looked over at us sullenly for a moment and frowned.

He walked over and introduced himself. "I'm Special Agent Hampton FBI, Is Rex in?"

I pointed to the front door of the lodge. I wondered why he seemed to know Rex by his first name. Lubinski met him at the door and they disappeared inside.

The agent's glare had stuck in my craw. I thought about it for a moment and looked at Mike, his hair was hanging over his ears, his beard was a week old, and his ball cap was on backwards. He looked as skuzzy as I felt. I decided to take the agent's scowl as a compliment given the role we were playing.

"You know," Mike said in a hushed tone. "We're in the perfect place to nail Jimmy on the rape right now. I feel bad that we weren't here to prevent it from happening but if Jimmy goes with us on a drive this afternoon, I'm gonna ask him about it."

After a while, Hampton walked out, got in his truck and gave us a dismissive wave and drove off.

Rex came out and walked over to us.

"What was that all about?" Mike asked.

"It's about that thing with Jimmy, I didn't tell him a thing," Rex claimed. "Why don't you go take Jimmy hunting? It'll make him feel better if he kills something."

"Since when does the FBI get involved in rapes?" I asked.

"This place is within the rez even though it's private ground, and Jimmy is an Indian, so they gotta stick their nose in it."

"You mean there's an FBI office in Orofino?" Mike asked.

"No, he's from Lewiston."

"Well," Mike said, "To hell with all this Five-O stuff, let's go get Jimmy and see whether we can't get us a moose."

"You guys go grab him," Rex said. "I'll stay here in case somebody else shows up."

We drove to Jimmy's trailer. He was still wearing the same clothes we'd seen him in all week but at least he seemed cheerful to see us. I assumed he had been given the opportunity to shower at the jail, but it didn't appear he'd taken advantage of it. He gathered his rope, rifle, and axe, and we loaded up. I got in the middle and Jimmy rolled in next to me and confirmed my no-shower theory.

"Let's run into town and get some beer," Jimmy said. "I'll pay you back when I get the money for that elk."

We drove into 'Fino, stopped at the convenience store and Mike ran in and got another case of Budweiser. Jimmy was dry, he opened one up and drank several swallows.

Charbonneau suggested we head towards Pierce. Mike asked him to navigate and we turned upriver on Highway 12. Mike pointed across the river. "Looky there, a bald eagle."

"There's one that guards my grandfather's grave not too far from here," Jimmy stated. "If you want, I can kill it and make a tail-feather fan, I get a couple of hundred bucks for 'em."

Mike turned towards him. "Donny's the one that's interested in that stuff; I'll ask him."

We turned off the highway and onto a bridge that crossed the Clearwater and drove into the tiny town of Greer. The paved two lane road stayed in the bottom through town and started climbing up the canyon. On top, we crossed rolling hills of farm fields sprinkled with stands of conifers. I pointed to a road sign indicating we were nine miles out of Weippe.

"Jimmy," I asked. "How the hell you pronounce that?"

"We-wipe-too, but we don't brag about it," he laughed.

He was in a good mood—glad to be going somewhere and drinking beer again. Mike caught the moment and asked the million dollar question.

"Jimmy," Mike glanced at him. "Did you really screw that little girl?"

Jimmy lowered his voice and said, "No, but I stuck my finger in her."

We had him. Two officers could testify to Charbonneau's admission of L & L which was lewd and

lascivious conduct with a minor. The only remorse I
sensed from him was that of getting caught.

We rode on in silence for a few minutes, and Mike
spoke up again. "Jimmy, Donny says he's got a friend in
Missoula that would like to buy an elk. Are you
interested?"

"How long's he known this guy?" Jimmy asked.

"I asked him the same question. They went to school
together. A long time."

"Sure," Jimmy answered. "But he'll probably have to
come and get it."

"I gotta come back through on my route in a couple of
weeks, we might be able to just drive over there and give
it to him."

"That'd work too."

Weippe was about twice the size of Greer. It had both
a Post Office and a gas station along with a few idle
logging trucks. The road turned north, and we switched
from farm fields to forest. There had been light traffic
between the two bergs, but since we'd left Weippe traffic
diminished to next to nothing.

We drove another ten miles and started into Pierce,
just before Main Street, Jimmy pointed at a side road
and said, "Let's go out French Creek, we should find
something out there."

And after about ten miles we did. A black cow moose
was standing fifty yards off the paved road in the timber.
"Let's just go on up a ways," Jimmy said while watching
the moose. "We can turn around and come back. That
way's I don't have to get out of the truck. I don't wanna
spook it."

Mike drove about three hundred yards and turned around. Jimmy stuck the barrel out the window and chambered a round. I grabbed the video camera off the dash and got it rolling.

"Slow down—I think she's right in here somewhere," Jimmy said.

She hadn't moved. She'd probably grown up watching traffic driving by, but this was no day to stand and gawk. We could only see her head, neck, and the top of her back in the dense timber. Jimmy brought the rifle up and Mike shut the truck off.

"I hope it's a little one," Jimmy said, peering into the scope.

And then, the rifle roared and the moose dropped into the vegetation. A second moose moved into view to its right.

"Oh, fuck, I got the momma, goddamn it," Jimmy said.

I got the distinct impression that Jimmy had wanted the calf that was just short of a year old and not the full sized adult cow.

"How do you want to do this, Jimmy?" I asked.

"I'll go up there and you guys go ride around for a little bit," he replied.

"I'll go up there and give you a hand," I offered.

"Grab my hatchet and rope from the back," Jimmy instructed. "I'd better take the rifle up there though."

I threw the coiled rope over my shoulder and picked up his axe and walked up carrying the camera.

The moose was down where she had fallen, her chest was heaving for air. Last-year's calf stood fifty yards away staring.

"I think she's still alive, Jimmy."

Jimmy ejected the spent cartridge case from the rifle, put it in his pants pocket and racked a new round into the chamber. He was breathing as if he'd just run a 100-meter dash, and it took him a minute to catch his breath, all while the cow's chest was racking up and down ten yards away.

Jimmy walked to the uphill side of the moose. He had his axe in his right hand and the .243 in his other. He reached out one-handed and held the muzzle a few inches from the animal's head. Wham! The rifle recoiled and the moose contracted, its legs kicking in its last wished-for run.

Jimmy turned around and looked at the calf that was still gaping at us. For a second, I thought he might shoot it too. Instead, he laid the rifle down, took the sheath off the axe and stuck it in his back pocket. He blew his nose into the vegetation and began chopping. I wasn't sure if the animal was dead. With each whack she kicked—a part of her was still struggling to get away.

Jimmy finished the beheading, opened up the abdominal cavity with his folding knife and cut the diaphragm exposing the chest cavity. He picked the axe back up and chopped through the sternum, reached in and severed the trachea and esophagus. He grabbed the two tubes and pulled out the heart and lungs; the liver and digestive track followed.

The cow's amniotic sac was full of a failed promise. I pulled out my pocketknife and cut the sack open exposing the calf. I could clearly see the pulse pounding through the little animal's wet chest. It was horrifying. I picked the camera back up and caught the beating of the heart for the sake of prosecution. I couldn't do anything for the little guy but try to see that it got its day in court. I stepped back and caught the whole scene on tape. The tiny calf lay dying in the foreground. Momma's steaming organs piled next to it, and her split-open carcass lying on its back above the guts. It was *the* classic reason for not allowing hunting in the spring. It was *the* reason to put a stop to Charbonneau and Lubinski's killing.

Jimmy finished eviscerating the cow. He sat back and gasped for air. I sat down with him. "What time does it get dark, Jimmy?"

"About six I think."

"How many moose you get in a year?"

"Ten or twelve," Jimmy stated.

"You gonna cut it in half?"

"Yeah, while it's still light."

Jimmy cut the moose in two by cutting behind the rib cage and through the spinal column with both the knife and axe. He tied half hitches around one hind leg, and another knot around a front leg so the two halves were joined to the rope. There had been no traffic pass along the road while we were at the kill scene and if there had been, there was too much vegetation for us to be seen.

Mike pulled up and stopped. Jimmy appeared to be thinking whether or not it would be safe to try to get the

moose out during daylight. He stood up, waved at Mike
and turned to me, "Lets do it."

Jimmy grabbed the rope and axe and began moving
to the road feeding coils as he walked. I picked up his
rifle and noted the bolt's striker was forward, indicating
an empty chamber.

Jimmy tied the rope to the trailer hitch below the
bumper and told "Pate" to drive until the moose was on
the road. The truck lurched forward, the rope came tight,
and the two moose-halves bounced down through the
timber and sprang around the trees. *There goes
momma,* I thought.

Mike backed up to the two halves, and we hurriedly
loaded them. I don't think our exposure on the road
lasted more than five minutes. I was disgusted with how
easy it had been to pull off the illegal killing of a moose
in broad daylight on a paved road. But our killer was
caught; he just didn't know it yet.

We jumped back in the truck, all three of us
breathing hard. Jimmy grabbed a beer, popped the top,
and drank a big gulp down between breaths.

"That was amazing," I said.

"That was like a surgical extraction," Mike added.
"How long did it take you to perfect that?"

"I've been doing it about six years now, I guess."

We drove on down the road back to Pierce and off the
plateau at Greer. When we hit, the highway, Jimmy told
Mike to turn up towards Kamiah and explained that he
wanted to give half the moose to Tom. We pulled into the
trailer court. Tom was drinking with a half dozen other
people under an open woodshed. They were all lit up,

and it wasn't from our headlights. Jimmy and Mike got out and dumped the front half of the moose on the ground. We spent about ten minutes making man-cracks with the group and drinking beer. A taller half-blood asked me whether I wanted to buy a set of moose horns.

"I'll pass," I said.

The guy produced a large set of moose antlers from behind the shed and said, "Forty-dollars."

"I'll take 'em," I said and peeled two twenty-dollar bills from my wallet. I set my beer on the truck hood and loaded the antlers in the back. I came back around, picked up my beer and toasted the seller.

"I'm Tony Henderson," I said.

"Leonard Charbonneau."

Unlawful sale of moose antlers by a tribal member, I thought to myself.

We said *adios* to the group, and the three of us squeezed back into the truck. Jimmy Charbonneau hadn't lost any weight in the few minutes we'd been out.

"How's that guy related to you?" I asked.

"He's another cousin."

Mike turned onto Highway 12 and followed the Clearwater down towards Orofino. The headlights illuminated a rocky spot along the river, and Jimmy said, "If I ever catch that fucking Bill Snow alone, I'm gonna cut him up into little pieces and throw them right down there and let the birds eat him."

I didn't hear it as an idle threat; he was serious. Given the opportunity, Jimmy Charbonneau would kill Snow just as dead as the moose.

There was a pause in the conversation, and then Mike asked, "Who you talking about, Jimmy?"

"Snow, the game warden. He lives in 'Fino," Jimmy snapped. "That's his rock we pee on all the time."

We pulled into the road going into Jimmy's trailer, and Mike looked over at Charbonneau. "What are you doing tomorrow night Jimmy? We'd like to take you and Tom to dinner in Lewiston, get a good meal and square up with you; celebrate."

"That sounds good, sure," Jimmy replied.

We unloaded Jimmy's gear and beer and drove off for the lodge.

"What was that all about?" I asked. "Dinner in Lewiston? Jimmy doesn't even eat real food."

"To begin with we need to do some wining and dining with these crooks, but more important, if Lube's lodge is on the rez, we'd better make sure we pay these Indians *off* the rez to get this thing into county court 'cause the tribe ain't going to do a damn thing," Mike explained.

I felt ignorant. I had not thought about the fact that we should be paying tribal members off the reservation, I hadn't worked much involving tribal members, certainly nothing within a reservation, and dealing with Indian law was new to me. The killing had been committed off-reservation, but the element of sale needed to be articulated off-reservation to ensure a clean prosecution in state court.

Mike went on to explain that Charbonneau had told him he had clients in Missoula. "So," Mike paused. "If we can give him the opportunity to sell some meat to Burke. And he takes us up on it. We might be able to figure out how to deliver fish or meat for him to some of his other clients. Besides, it would be good to have a charge against him in Montana and it sounds as if he's interested."

We passed Snow's Rock without peeing. Both of us were thinking about what Charbonneau had said about killing Bill Snow. It was clear that if Jimmy Charbonneau figured out who we really were at the wrong time it would probably be lethal. He seemed comfortable with us for the moment, and I believed I had built trust with him by assisting in the church burglary. Mike seemed to have bonded with him by using his smooth gift of gab and promise of money.

Mike pulled into the Crabtree, backed up to the garage, and we hung the hindquarters of the moose next to the doe. Rex greeted us with a smile and nodded at the moose.

"Got Donny's black walnuts I see," he gushed. "Where'd you get it?"

"Out by French Creek," I replied.

Mike added, "Hey, tomorrow night I want to take everybody out to dinner in Lewiston. I'll buy you, Jimmy, and Tom a good meal and square up."

"Well, we can do that," Rex smiled.

"Maybe you can get a hold of Tom and round the two of them up tomorrow then," Mike added. "And make sure to tell Tom that I'll pay him tomorrow night for the fish, too. Donny wants it all."

It was late and well past dinner time. Mike and I helped us to some leftovers and hit the sack. Mike whispered over to me, "Let's go to Lewiston tomorrow and see whether we can't find that FBI agent."

Chapter 15

Breaking Bread

The next morning without planning to, I slept until nine. I walked down to the main floor of the lodge. There was an unknown younger female drinking coffee and with Mike and Rex. I grabbed a mug, and Rex introduced me. "Tony, this is Kristy, my mistress."

My mind was doing mental eye-rolls inside my cranium again. *Only Lube,* I thought. I was sure I had never heard anyone use the word mistress except as a joke.

Kristy had a mousy face, shoulder length dishwater blonde hair and was drug-skinny. She wore pink sweatpants, a gray tank top, and obviously no bra. A cigarette hung from her hips. Undeniably she had spent the night.

Mike set the stage for our trip to Lewiston. He'd told Rex that we were going to drive down to the hospital at Lewiston so he could set up an account at the hospital with their purchasing office.

I helped myself to some cold eggs and sausage and sat down with the crew. Kristy was ditzy. She wanted to talk about the moose we had gotten the night before, and I scowled at Lube. He got the message.

"You don't know nothing about no moose," he told her.

"Moose?" she sniggered. "I don't even know nothing about that moose we got before Christmas, neither," She smiled and lit another cigarette.

Rex nodded approvingly at her.

Mike and I grabbed a cup of coffee for the road and headed out the door. Driving down the Ahsahka Grade, we talked about what we'd tell the FBI and how it would affect our investigation. We both agreed that Charbonneau's admission to the lewd act had set things in motion. He would be charged, and sooner or later he would learn that his statement he'd made to us would be used to prosecute him.

"Don't worry about it," Mike explained. "Federal court is much slower than state court. Jimmy-C won't have his first court appearance on his sexual assault until late fall at the earliest. It shouldn't cause us any problems and I'll make sure this FBI guy keeps us in the loop."

There was no question in my mind that what Charbonneau had done to the girl was a higher priority than any wildlife case, but I felt a deep need to see justice for the wild victims, too. It was our job to be the advocates for wildlife, we'd let the FBI lead the charge for Trudy.

Thirty minutes later we were knocking on a locked glass door in an office suite. The glass was reinforced with wire. Painted on the glass in gold were the words: Federal Bureau of Investigation, U.S. Department of Justice. Hampton looked up from his desk, gave us a quizzical expression, walked over and let us in. We introduced ourselves using our real names for a change and told him what we were up to. Hampton's demeanor did a one-eighty and his face relaxed.

Mike took the lead and told him what Charbonneau had admitted to the previous day.

Hampton lit up. "That should close the door on him. I'm still planning on bringing him in for a follow-up interview, but as you know it's good to have the answers before you ask the questions. I'll work out a theme of minimizing the crime using the finger angle without burning you guys—he might just roll over on himself and give it up."

Hampton paused and continued. "I've been up to Lubinski's before. It was a case on Jimmy's brother last year."

"You mean Basil?" I asked.

"No, it was Norman. I think he's younger than Jimmy. He shot his girlfriend in the head with a thirty-thirty at Lubinski's lodge last summer."

"You're kidding me," I exclaimed.

"No, I'm not," Hampton stated. "It was right out there in front where you guys were. It didn't kill her, it just grazed the outside of her skull."

"He's in prison?" I asked.

"No, my office burned down last year, the rifle was destroyed in the fire and the victim claimed she didn't remember the shooting. So we didn't have a case against him. He walked. Lubinski wasn't any help."

"Arson?" I inquired.

"We couldn't determine what started it," Hampton scowled. It was obvious he had his own theory but he didn't elaborate.

I told him about Basil raping Tom's girlfriend in Kamiah.

"Quite the clan. I'll bounce it off the tribal cops to see whether they've heard anything, but unless she wants to step forward and talk about it, it's not gonna happen. It's hard enough to charge a rape when there's no physical evidence, but it's impossible when the vic won't report it. Working with these people is frustrating, they aren't like you and me; they're different. Most of them are fine people, but many of them would rather handle things themselves than report it, especially when it involves family members."

I told Hampton about the church.

"We've got jurisdiction over burglaries in Indian Country, but it's the same problem I just mentioned; the U.S. Attorney's office won't go after a case where the victim won't cooperate. The Charbonneau's aren't big on law enforcement as you've probably figured out, I'll bet Basil is gonna want to take care of it himself—and it could turn into a pile of dog shit that I have to clean up."

"Were you the guy that Jimmy attacked with the rock?" I asked.

"No, that happened before I got here. At least he did some time over it."

Hampton promised to keep our information secure for now, and we promised to send him copies of our reports. As we were leaving, Mike brought up our planned dinner and asked for restaurant ideas.

"Take 'em to Bojack's. I'll make sure my wife and I don't eat there tonight," he laughed and paused. His face got serious, and he lowered his voice. "You guys be careful."

We ate lunch, and Mike wanted to walk through the Lewiston hospital "in the event Rex quizzes us about it." Mike stopped at US Bank and got several hundred dollars for the planned payoff. He'd decided to make the payments in cash since Charbonneau had been suspicious of the last undercover investigator when he'd insisted on giving him a check. I doubted Jimmy had an easy way to cash one anyway. I couldn't imagine he had a bank account. We did the hospital walk-through, headed over to Bojack's, looked at the menu, and made reservations.

Mike smiled at me and said, "You watch, Roger's going to have a shit-fit over this dinner bill."

I looked around the interior; it was a bit on the uppity side. It was the polar opposite of the watering hole in Orofino. This was a place you would take somebody special and we had special guests—even if they weren't the typical customers that Bojack's catered to. I could see Mike's angle on this idea, but *this was going to be embarrassing,* I thought, *being with these yahoos in here.*

We decided to run up to Lisa Gardiner's and pick up the deer antlers. Mike turned up the Potlatch River to Kendrick, cut over to Cavendish and down to her trailer house. It was a route I hadn't seen since my college days.

Lisa met us at the door. She was wearing dark glasses and her face was puffy. She was submissive and unsociable. We followed her over to her shop. She climbed on a ladder and retrieved the antlers from a rafter. She'd mounted them on particleboard veneered with oak and had covered the skull plate with brown felt. I counted out $60 and didn't bother asking for a receipt. She carried the antlers out to the truck. I opened up the camper door and dropped the tailgate which was painted with dried blood and flecked moose hairs. She laid the antlers in the back without a comment. We thanked her and left.

As Mike and I drove off, we talked about what we had against Gardiner and compared her case to the cases involving Lubinski and the Charbonneaus. It was obvious she was a crooked taxidermist, but we were neck-deep with our main targets. We both agreed we were probably done with Lisa. We had bigger fish to fry. It would be up to Snow and Squires to figure out whether to pursue anything on her.

We'd managed to drag our feet enough to avoid the lodge until sundown. Rex had picked up Jimmy and Tom, and the three of them were sitting in the living room drinking Keystone. There was no sign of Kristy. Rex had changed into a clean western shirt, and Tom had cleaned up too. However, Jimmy was still wearing the same clothes and had his signature black ball cap on backwards. His odor hung on his three hundred and thirty pounds like fog on a mountain. At least he appeared sober.

"I got reservations for us at Bojack's in an hour."

"Oh, we don't have to go to that place," Rex spoke up, "That's too damn fancy."

"No," Mike declared. "I insist. You guys have been good to us and we need to consummate our friendships.

I always take my clients to dinner; it's part of business,"
Mike paused and smiled. "I'll write it off on my expense
account," and then he laughed. "Just like these black
walnuts and red potatoes."

We loaded into Mike's rig. Big Jimmy got in front. I
crawled into the back with Rex and Tom and the
mounted deer antlers. *We'll be wearing moose hair,* I
thought. The top of the camper shell was just inches
above my head; the metal bed was hard and cold. I was
getting tired of riding in the back of Mike's truck, but it
was "sixes" since being cramped into the front next to
Jimmy wasn't fun either.

The three of us were sitting in the back not saying
much, the noise really too loud for conversation and I
was trying to come up with something I could talk about
to smoke out an inculpatory tidbit.

"Does Kristy hunt at all?" I asked Rex.

"Well not really, she buys a deer tag every year but
her brothers usually fill it. She went out with me this
winter when I killed that little bull moose, though."

Bingo, I thought, *we have a witness to the moose
shooting.* At breakfast, she'd said she'd been there, and
now he'd just given me the same story. We'd just have to
figure out Kristy's last name.

"Was that the yearling?" I asked.

"Yeah, we were able to put the entire thing in the
back of my Gremlin," he bragged.

Having driven his mobile pigsty, I was positive there
would still be moose hair in among the trash when we
took the case down; I made a mental note to include the
Gremlin under the umbrella of the search warrant.

I thought about what we had on *this* moose charge. We had his story, plus Tina at the lab had confirmed he had provided us moose meat. Now, we had the first name of a witness, and I knew we'd find the hair in the car to corroborate it. It was starting to look like a damn good case.

"I thought maybe she'd come with us tonight," I said.

"No, I sent her home with my car this afternoon. She's moving in with me though. I'm not gonna to charge her for room, but I'll give her a bill so she can turn it into welfare and get some money."

"She live in 'Fino?" I asked.

"No she lives in Weippe. Her dad's the Homelite dealer but she's tired of living with her folks."

"She looks a bit old to be living with her parents," I laughed.

"She's thirty-two; she moved back in with her folks after breaking up with some asshole."

I'd get "the Snow man" working on the information, and I was sure he'd have a source in Weippe that could give us her last name.

Mike found a place to park in town. We unloaded and the five of us walked into Bojack's. The restaurant was downstairs, and its companion bar was at street level. The receptionist said our table would be ready in a few minutes, and she suggested we sit in the bar. The place was noisy. Mike ordered five Budweisers from the waitress. I poured my beer in a glass that was sitting on the table. We looked like escapees from the Jet Club, but nobody seemed to notice.

Halfway through the beer the waitress moved us downstairs to our table. The dining room was smaller than the bar and although it was full it was more restrained, there was a hush about it. The beer loosened me up, and I thought about my earlier concerns of being embarrassed to be seen with this crew and I shrugged it off.

I looked at my menu, and I turned to Jimmy, "Are you going to eat anything tonight? You should have a big beef steak on Pate."

"No, I'm just gonna drink beer," he said with a yellow-toothed smile.

The waitress seemed blind to our slovenliness. We ordered four steaks from rare to medium. I had to bite my lip when she asked whether we wanted a bottle of wine with our entrees.

The four of us ate our food, and Jimmy sucked his down. There wasn't much chatter other than how we liked our steaks. After the waitress cleared the table Mike brought out his fat wallet and turned to Jimmy. "There's thirteen sacks of steelhead from the other night. Donny said he'd take it all. Tom said you'd let 'em go for twelve bucks a sack. That's a hundred and sixty bucks. Have we got a deal?"

Jimmy looked down at the wallet in Mike's hand. "Yeah, sure," he said enthusiastically.

"Okay, here's four twenties for you Jimmy, and here's yours, Tom," Mike paused and turned back to Jimmy. "Donny still wants a hundred pounds of moose, and when I talked to him today he said he'd take another hundred pounds off that cow we got yesterday—if that's okay?" Mike paused looking at Jimmy. "So that would be another six hundred at three bucks a pound, right?"

"That sounds good to me," Jimmy purred.

Mike was dealing cash out as though we were playing seven card stud. I looked around, assuming every person in the room would be staring, but nobody seemed to be paying attention. We were the elephant in the room.

On the way back to Orofino, Lubinski became talkative and unloaded a bit. He brought up the fact that Jimmy owed him money over the meat. As he put it, "Jimmy and I have a deal," he complained. "I've burned up a lot of gas using my rig. I was the one that brokered this thing and got it going, and he owes me for that too."

He quit whining about Jimmy and brought up his favorite subject, prostitution. "I talked to a retired whore about what I want to do at the lodge, and she said I needed to have some protection."

"What do you mean, protection"? I asked.

"Security. I'd need to have security for the whores. I'll need to have some big bouncer guy."

I wasn't interested in finding out the details of his whorehouse plans so I didn't quiz him on it any further. The silence was broken by Tom's greed. "I'll take you whitetail hunting before the white man season. It'll cost a hundred and fifty a day plus a five-hundred dollar kill fee."

This coming from my drinking and thieving buddy, I thought. The money Mike had handed out tonight was like blood in the water—it was bringing in the sharks. I told him I'd think about it and looked at Rex. "Have you got any frozen moose I could take home tomorrow?"

"I've got a couple of thirty pounders in the freezer I can sell ya."

"One would be great."

That chatter got Tom talking again. "I can get more fish for you next fall if you want," he offered. "I've got two guys in Montana that comes over for steelhead, I get seven-fifty apiece. They won't come over for less than twenty per trip."

The information Tom had just given me was important. He'd made the initial offer to sell us the stolen fish so we didn't have an entrapment issue with him, but now we had information from him that sounded legitimate involving past trafficking. It was a statement, if need be, I could turn to a jury, look them in the eye and quote him.

Mike and I were up early the next morning. We wanted out. We'd been putting in long stressful days and we were both getting burned out. I felt dirty and buggy as if I were back chasing fires in Alaska.

Rex fed us breakfast. He promised to get the elk and moose meat frozen and packaged for shipping to Donny. Again, he complained about Jimmy owing him money. Last night was still grinding on him; he'd gotten a steak dinner out of it but hadn't gotten the cash his co-conspirator had made off with. I rolled out $90 in green for the moose meat he'd promised me and he perked up. We went out to the garage, pulled a sack labeled "30#-M" and put it in my cooler.

"I don't think he wanted to say anything to you, but Pate's hoping you'll make out receipts for the meat you're sending down to Donny," I stated. "It'd help him on his taxes."

As I expected, he was amiable about the idea. I grabbed the moose antlers I'd bought from Leonard Charbonneau and loaded them in the back of the truck next to the deer antlers. When we returned to the dining room, Mike told him about Donny's "friend" in Missoula who wanted an elk and Rex said it would be okay to give him the lodge's phone number. I made it clear that I had to get back to my smokejumping job in Fairbanks and promised Rex I would steal a cargo parachute for him so he could use it as a party canopy outside his lodge.

Mike made out a check to Rex for $472 to cover lodging and meals—$360 for the room and $112 for wild-game meals.

Lubinski made out a receipt for the meat he'd shipped to California and gave it to Mike. It claimed he'd sold a hundred pounds of potatoes for $300. *Damn expensive spuds,* I thought. He made another receipt out for thirty-pounds of black walnuts for $90 and handed it to me.

We thanked him, jumped in Mike's rig and headed down the road. We both felt good. Happy to be out of Lube's world and ecstatic about what we'd accomplished on our third trip to the Land of the Bill Snow Rock.

Mike called his boss from a pay phone in Grangeville, knowing that Roger would have to be stoked by what we had pulled off. I stood next to Mike as he went into detail about the Swamp Creek deer, the Three Bears elk, the church burglary, the French Creek moose, the pending sale to Montana and the fish we'd bought from the burglary. He finished his briefing with the telling of dinner at Bojacks.

I leaned in close and heard Roger's one comment. "I'm glad you guys are safe, but you two spent more on that dinner than our travel policy allows." Mike's smile fizzled into a frown. "I'll talk to you about it in the office this week sometime," and hung up. We were both demoralized. We'd worked our butts off and taken risks that could have gotten us killed—Roger's comment had taken our spark.

Chapter 16

Bureaucratic Courage

The trip home wasn't any shorter than the previous trip. During the drive, I thought about the Nez Perce I'd met in the last months. When I'd fought fire in Alaska prior to becoming a warden, I'd had many experiences with Athabascan Indian firefighters. I'd found them friendly with a great sense of humor—both traits had really helped when times were tough on the fire line. They shared their bug-dope, coats, and stew. If I'd walk into a group of them speaking their native tongue, they'd switch to English out of courtesy. Curiously, Athabascans demonstrated their wealth by giving their possessions away during potlatches. I'd stumbled upon this when the entire village of Tanacross had burnt to the ground. I think there had been about 30 small log cabins with sod roofs and chinked with moss that had been lost. None had plumbing or electricity. Each had a white plywood outhouse that had escaped the fire and gave the scene a larger-than life grave-yard impression. Looking at a pile of ash that had been someone's home, I noticed the charred remains of numerous Winchester lever-action rifles. When I asked a stricken tribal member about it, she explained that the owner of the cabin had been planning a potlatch and that during the event the new rifles, along with several Hudson Bay blankets, would have been given away. The other impressive strength within their culture was their glue-like sense of family. It didn't seem to matter if a person were a sibling or a distant cousin. They were all blood, and they stuck together. Certainly Jimmy and Tom were sticking together but the fact that Basil had raped his son's lady was hard to swallow. I decided that Mike and I'd fallen in with a bad crowd from two cultures.

I stopped at the kennel on the way through Salmon and picked Ben up. I was pumped to see him, and he was flat-out enthralled to have me back. His nose focused on the odors buried in my Levi's, and I knew he smelled the dead animals from the trip. What other story his nose revealed was a puzzle to me, but I'm sure it was a good read. I put him up front in my patrol vehicle. He laid his head on the wooden seat-box with his brown eyes facing me and was stroked for twenty-one miles. I pulled into my driveway past North Fork. We'd had a sprout of green-up while I'd been gone and the place looked and smelled crisp. I turned on my answering machine as an assertion that I was back to my norm. No Keystone, no laughing at humorless jokes, no skuzzy bars, no truck-bed rides, and best of all; no lying. It was remarkable to be home.

The next morning I called my boss in Salmon. I let him know I was back and that I had evidence that needed to be sent to the lab, a twenty plus-page report that needed writing, and investigative leads that needed to be chased down. He didn't ask any questions, and I didn't offer any details. I wondered if somebody at headquarters hadn't had a heart-to-heart with him over the leak.

My next call was to Mike. We'd talked about my
Alaska smokejumper cover before our last trip to Orofino
and both agreed it was problematic. Our first contact
with Lube had been three months ago, and neither one of
us had foreseen this case going as long as it had. If
Henderson were a real Fairbanks jumper, he needed to
get back to work. We talked about our options with my
cover. We had two choices, either Henderson would have
to quit the job or he needed to get his butt back to work.
We decided on the latter. The winter snow pack had been
drought-like and the snowline was much higher than it
should have been for April. These factors were setting
the West up for an early fire season. With such a pending
fire prediction, it would be normal to move jumpers from
Fairbanks to the fire center in Boise. We'd just have to
tweak my cover so I could resurface in June. But for now,
I was benched and it left Mike hanging. If he went back
to Orofino before "Henderson's" return, he'd have to do
it alone.

Mike told me that he had just gotten off the phone
with Gary Burke in Montana discussing the facilitation of
a "buy" in Missoula. They had talked it over at length,
and it was no surprise to Mike or me that Burke had
embraced the idea. Mike had already thrown the idea out
to Lubinski and Charbonneau, and they were both
interested. Mike would set up another visit to the
Crabtree in a couple of weeks, facilitate the hunt and
hopefully take Charbonneau and a dead elk to Missoula
to sell to Burke.

During the last trip to Orofino, we'd developed
information that the volume of game animals and fish

being trafficked out of the area was much greater than we had originally figured. Bill Snow probably had a grasp about it from his years embedded in the community, but Mike and I had both been naive about it. We were troubled by our facilitation of Charbonneau's carnage during this last trip; however, we agreed that it would have occurred whether we had been there or not—and the only way of stopping his many-year spree was to bring a voluminous case before a judge and let him administer justice by putting our two primary targets behind bars. Regretfully the only way Mike and I could see terminating this pattern of trafficking was that other animals were going to have to die, and at least one was destined for Missoula.

Mike had also talked to his boss, "Roger the Bean Counter," as I had begun to refer to him; Roger was concerned with my participation in the burglary, and I reminded Mike it was either jump in or allow an extremely drunken driver loose on the road. Mike was aware of this and had emphasized it to him. But, Roger had a hard time thinking outside normal game warden patrol (such as an untagged deer). He'd been a good field warden in his day and had gained a reputation for being able to sort through a cooler of fish, question the anglers, and come up with "the who caught what." What he lacked was undercover experience and it was showing.

Roger had decided that the investigation had gotten convoluted to the point that the director's office needed to be briefed. Mike explained to me that Roger had also said he was uncomfortable with the sexual assaults, the FBI's involvement, and the fact that the case would probably become politically sensitive with the tribe. This got my blood boiling. If Roger really wanted to know about being uncomfortable, he should go for a ride with Jimmy, or fish with dope-smoking Mickey, or maybe have a few beers in the Jet Club with our pals. But I kept my vent shut; I knew Mike had the same frustration and I suspected him of watering down Roger's comments.

Roger had set the director's briefing for the following week in Boise, and he wanted both of us there. Mike suggested that it would be good timing for the two of us to try to meet with the prosecutor in Orofino the following day. I really wanted to just stay home with my dog, but it wasn't meant to be. The Boise briefing wasn't optional, and we really needed to get the prosecutor up to speed.

My third call was to Snow. I told him that Mike would be calling him to try to set up a meeting with his prosecutor and that I needed to chase down the last name of Lube's girlfriend (or mistress). I ran through the story and when I mentioned that her father was the Homelite dealer in Weippe he interrupted.

"Yeah, a cup of coffee says it's going to be Kristy Washer. Eastman's been chasing her brothers for a while."

Bill brought up the burglary. He thought it was a no-brainer on my participation but strongly believed that Sheriff Albers needed to know about it.

"Tony, he's been a friend of mine for years, and if you can trust anybody, it's Nick Albers. We really need to let him know about it so somebody doesn't accuse you of being a crook."

The last thing I needed was allegations that I had crossed over to the dark side. I gave Bill my endorsement; it was good having the old Marine watching our backs.

I needed to get a sample from the moose meat that Lube had sold me. It was still frozen and wrapped in a white plastic bag that Lube had taped tightly. It was labeled with a black marker, "30# -M." I photographed it and removed the wrapper and photographed it again. I went out to the garage, took my meat saw off the wall and wet the blade with bleach and washed it off using the outside hose bib. I went back inside and sliced a small V of frozen meat out of the slab and bagged and tagged the sample. I put it in my freezer and placed the thirty pounds in a fresh garbage bag and wired it shut with a second numbered evidence tag and jotted down the two evidence numbers for my report.

I pulled a clean short-sleeved gray uniform shirt out of my closet, mounted my badge, and name tag on it and put it on. I was jumping the gun a bit with the short sleeves, but I had the fever. I loaded Ben into the truck bed, and we headed to the office with the remainder of the meat. It was good to be back in my marked truck wearing the uniform and gun belt.

I put the meat in the evidence freezer and added the information onto the evidence log attached to the clipboard. I glanced around inside and noted the elk quarters were gone, and I assumed they had been butchered and distributed to some hard-luck family. The sheep head was still staring blankly.

The freezer butted next to a large Quonset hut filled
with myriads of old gear, there was everything from deer
drive-nets to electro-shock fishing contrivances. It was
quite the accumulation, and it was always a fascinating
poke-through. During one of my previous exploratory
forays into its depths, I'd located two para-cargo
parachutes packed in their heavy canvas containers. I
figured the department had obtained them in some ill
thought out surplus equipment purchase. Back in my fire
days, I'd been the recipient of many para-cargo drops
and knew that if you didn't know what you were doing
(as in a *real* smokejumper), the chutes would get you
killed if you actually tried to use them for their intended
job. The department now had a purpose for one of the
'chutes; I'd use it to enhance my cover. I would be the
department's first covert operative to use a parachute on
a case—so to speak. I took one of the chutes and threw it
in my truck.

When I got home, I sat down at my desk; it was time
to write the report. Just thinking about it was
intimidating. We'd been undercover for six nights and
six full days, and each had its own oddness. The one
good thing about writing case reports is that they're
chronological. I began typing about the night we arrived,
and details started rushing back. Day two was easy also;
there was the scene at the hatchery with the Indians
snagging, Jimmy's mention of steelhead numbers, and
Lube's beer can thrown into the rocks. The Swamp Creek
trip was simple, I plugged the video camera into my TV
and watched the footage: My memory filled in the gaps
not caught on tape. The same with the second day

involving the early morning trip out to Three Bears with Charbonneau, followed by the flashback memory of Jimmy's undercover announcement. It went on for three days of typing. I called Mike and read it back to him. He kept breaking in with details that I had forgotten. I let it sit for a day or two, added Mike's notes and reread it before declaring it finished. Putting the week's events on paper was a good way for me to accept the beast and let the memory lay.

I called up the sheriff's office and ran the license plate from the car that Earl had been driving when he bought the stolen fish. It was registered to Earl Lanolin. I picked up the phone and ordered a copy of Lanolin's driver's license photo to confirm he was indeed the Earl I had met. While on the line, I also ordered a driver's license photo of Kristy Washer.

Mike had gotten the phone number off the sheet that Charbonneau had used to call his egg buyer. I ran it through a reverse directory, and it showed the number belonged to a Shawn Livingston of Tensed. I called up our warden in Moscow, officer Clint Rand, and asked him whether he knew the guy.

"Yeah, I got a tip on him about an illegal elk a couple of years ago. Whatcha working on?"

"You ever hear of him buying steelhead or salmon eggs?"

"Yeah he cures 'em and sells them packaged and frozen in bait shops for steelheaders."

"Where's he getting 'em from?"

"I think he buys a lot from the Indians. We've always treated fish eggs as if they are guts—it's not illegal to sell guts. What you got going?" he asked.

"Oh," I paused. "It's something I'm doing for Roger Jones. I'll tell you about it when I can."

Clint chuckled, and we talked game warden gossip. It was mainly about who was up to what, who would get the next promotion, and what patrol area the advancement would open up. Neither of us was interested in promoting since it would involve a move, but it was always engaging to watch the domino shuffle across the state one promotion would cause.

I hung up and thought about the eggs I had purchased for our so-called fishing trips. Eggs cured and dyed, which were probably caught by the Charbonneau brothers and processed by Shawn. I wished I'd kept the packaging to see whether they were made in Tensed. I didn't see us twisting this Shawn guy into our net (though he knew Jimmy's eggs were stolen) but it was curious that maybe I'd bought some of Jimmy's final product.

The next call I made was to Tina in Ashland. "I've got another sample of meat I need you to run for species, and I'm betting it's moose again."

"Is it from the same case you've been working on? We've been testing a lot of moose lately here, and it's odd, since it's not hunting season."

"Yeah, same case, probably a different moose though. Did California send meat samples that tested positive for moose too?"

"Yes! Don't tell me all these are related?"

"Yeah, they are. From what I can tell, they are from several different moose but we can only guess from how many. We've got a good idea but it's circumstantial," I explained.

"We've got a research program right now geno-typing Shiras Moose and hopefully by this time next year we'll be able to analyze samples using their DNA for matching characteristics. If we had it now, I could sure tell you how many individual moose you had."

"I wish we could, it'd sure help."

It was good to talk to someone that was intelligent, enthusiastic, and sounded attractive. It was too bad she lived on the other side of another state. I needed to find a girlfriend; I needed a relationship.

On Monday afternoon, I dropped Ben off at the kennel. Neither of us was happy about it, and it struck me that if I hardly had time for my dog, what made me think I had time for a relationship? I drove to Boise and had dinner with Mike's family. His wife cooked a great meal, and I didn't have to wonder if she'd washed her hands (or feel as though I needed to send samples to the lab). His three girls were bright and friendly. The two youngest were shy and reserved.

After the food Mike and I talked about tomorrow's briefing. He'd discussed it with Roger and had asked who all would be there. Mike explained to me that Bill Hammer, the department's assistant director, would apparently represent Director Jerry Conley who had another commitment. Hammer was a guy that I hadn't had much exposure to during my short career; however, he had a reputation for being a stern political operative for the department and if he'd had a sense of humor none of us had ever seen it. Roger had also said that Dwight Kilgore, the Regional Conservation Officer overseeing enforcement activities in the Clearwater Region would be there. Dwight was Snow's boss and had been a soft-spoken, amicable guy the few times I'd talked to him, but beyond that I didn't really know him. Roger (the Bean Counter) would be there, of course, and he'd thought that maybe Steve Goddard would sit in. Goddard was assigned to the department as legal counsel from the Attorney General's office. He was a little briefcase of a lawyer with the air of an insightful grandfather. He didn't speak unless he had something worth saying. When he spoke, I'd come to the conclusion that I should listen. I was aware that he'd represented the state on several federal court cases that involved Indian law and off-reservation treaty rights. He was known amongst the troops as a legal-beagle for wildlife.

The pending meeting, however, was stressing me for two reasons: First Mike and I were going to be the only two people in the room that had put any juice into the case and it had gotten inside us; secondly, and more seriously, was the widening of the loop; the number of people who were aware of the investigation would double, and thus the chances of another leak would increase. It was a fact that Mike and I were just going to have to swallow.

We also talked about the meeting in Orofino that Snow had set up with the prosecutor. I was nervous as a caged mink about it. Going into Orofino and being seen by one of our targets would be a disaster, especially if we didn't see them. Snow had thought this through and would sneak us in through a back door from the alley. We'd "stage" in a motel in Grangeville and keep our exposure in Orofino as limited as possible.

The next morning Mike and I drove together to headquarters. I asked him whether he'd talked to Roger about Jimmy's offer to kill a bald eagle, and sell a fan made from the tail feathers.

Mike shook his head. "Yeah, I talked to him about it but he doesn't want anything to do with the feds right now. If we went federal on anything we'd need to bring the Fish and Wildlife agent in and Roger doesn't want to do it."

"What the hell's going on?" I asked.

"I don't know. That federal agent Roger deals with seems to be a good guy. He's just got some bug up his butt about it."

We met Roger Jones and Dwight Kilgore in the enforcement office in the department's main building on Walnut Street. I grabbed a cup of coffee out of the pot and the four of us walked down the hall to the Grizzly Room and sat down. The room was secluded with no windows, and was just large enough for a stout table surrounded by a dozen hardwood chairs. The room was aptly named after the silvertip grizzly skin mounted on the wall opposite the entrance door. The bear's glass eyes stared down at me from its big head, framed by its front paws spiked with four-inch claws. Its gaze didn't dispel my anxiety. I felt nearly as out of place at headquarters as I had during my last Jet Club visit.

Bill Hammer walked in with Steve Goddard. Steve smiled and asked how I was doing; he was obviously interested in what was at hand. Hammer was as personable as a pickup truck. Roger started the briefing off by going over Bill Snow's initial intelligence that had initiated the investigation. Mike took it from there and went into detail on what had transpired during our three trips. When he brought up the church burglary Hammer shot me a nasty glance and turned back to Mike.

"Have you got receipts on all this meat you've been buying?" Hammer asked.

"As a matter of fact we have," Mike brightened.

It was a ludicrous question, and it reflected Hammer's lack of understanding of criminal investigations. Certainly in the narcotics world, no agency would ever expect undercovers to obtain receipts from drug dealers, and this case wasn't any different. It was clear that Hammer was less than enthused about the case.

"Someday," Goddard injected. "I'd like you guys to tell me how you got receipts. It must be quite a story." Goddard's statement and the twinkle in his eye hinted that we had a supporter.

"Bill," Kilgore announced with a sharp inflection. "I've been getting reports about tribal members doing this kinda crap since I moved to Lewiston, and this investigation is long overdue."

"I hear the same thing," Hammer declared. "But you'll have to turn the Indians over to be prosecuted by the tribe; they need to save face on this thing. I deal with the tribe a lot."

"No," Kilgore proclaimed. "We're not going to do that. The tribe won't do a damn thing with this; we're going to prosecute this in state court."

Hammer looked at Kilgore for a few seconds and let it lay.

Dwight Kilgore had shown his spine. He'd just stood up to one of the most powerful men in the department and told him how it would be. Politically, it was hazardous, but for the sake of wildlife, Kilgore had just stuck his career on the block. I was quite impressed. It was an act of bureaucratic courage.

Chapter 17

Bear Hunters

Mike and I had lunch with Roger and Dwight following the meeting. Dwight was enthusiastic about the case. He hadn't been in the loop until that morning and was tired of hearing about tribal members illegally selling wildlife. Roger bragged us up and I hung on each of his words; I wasn't sold on his sincerity but maybe I was wrong about the guy.

Our discussion turned to Hammer's reaction to the case. We were moderately optimistic about how it went, but apparently Hammer's main focus seemed to be what the case would do to the department's relationship with the Nez Perce Tribe and not the damage to the resource that was going on. The older wardens in the department didn't trust him. They believed he looked upon enforcement as the bastard child of wildlife management. When a ticket was issued to somebody who was politically connected, it was usually Hammer that dealt with it. Hammer's boss, Jerry Conley, didn't put up with shenanigans in the department and was famous for inviting an employee to breakfast and firing him during the meal. It was my limited experience with Conley that if a warden did his job, and did it well; Conley's support would be there. I just hoped that Hammer didn't twist the facts of the case when he briefed Conley, especially regarding the role I'd played in the burglary.

After lunch, I followed Mike in my patrol vehicle as far as the hatchery at McCall, then I jumped in with Mike. He'd swapped out his normal undercover rig for a different unmarked truck to lessen the chance of our being recognized. We drove the four hours north to Grangeville and checked into a motel an hour from Orofino. The odds of running into one of our crooked friends were slim, but there was no sense increasing our exposure. We ordered a pizza delivered to our room for dinner.

Mike called Burke and talked about the Montana angle. Burke would make himself available to be in Missoula the following week if the stars aligned and Jimmy killed an elk to sell.

The next morning we grabbed breakfast rolls and coffee from the motel and headed for Orofino. Snow had set up the meeting for 8:00 a.m. sharp. The earlier hour would lessen the chance of our drunken friends from being out and about. Mike pulled behind the prosecutor's office and parked. Snow was waiting in his personal rig, and he showed us to the back door.

Bill introduced us to Clearwater County Prosecutor John Swain. John was exuberant and friendly. He was in his late forties, heavyset with sandy hair and a rosy complexion. John explained that he handled the felony cases in the county and that he would assign this case to his assistant, Lee Squires. This was good news; Snow had spoken highly of Squires.

There was a knock on the door, and I stiffened. John hollered out, and a great big guy walked in wearing slacks and a dress shirt. It was Squires. Snow made the introductions and began the briefing by explaining the information he had received about the Crabtree. Mike took over and started describing our first trip. When he brought up Jimmy Charbonneau, Swain nodded and cut in.

"I knew Jimmy in High School," John said lowering his voice. "We played basketball together. I don't think the coach liked him much. Probably 'cause he was an Indian, and he never really let Jimmy play. Jimmy just sat on the bench, and I felt sorry for him."

Swain's manifestation of empathy for Charbonneau didn't bode well; at least he wouldn't directly prosecute the case. Squires sat and listened intently while Mike expanded on the story. Lee liked the case's jury appeal and the fact that the evidence was irrefutable. Prosecutors never like weak cases and this one was quite the opposite. Swain pointed out that since the church was on Indian ground he didn't have jurisdiction, and it would be up to the FBI; however, he promised to think about charging Lubinski with possession of the stolen property since he wasn't an Indian. Both prosecutors had agreed that my decision to drive the night of the burglary had been a good idea. I appreciated their perception. Mike explained the developing Missoula angle with the goal of sniffing out Charbonneau's Montana market. Squires supported the idea.

We handed over copies of our reports to Squires and shook hands with both attorneys. Squires' handshake was full of enthusiasm, but I didn't detect the same feeling from Swain. Mike and I snuck out the back door, slinked to our truck, and headed south. Nothing in the meeting had been extraordinary other than Swain's statement about knowing Charbonneau. Both of us were comfortable with Squires; he was on board and eager to prosecute. The tales of the killing and selling had gotten his focus.

On the way back to McCall, Mike said he'd call Lube and commit to visiting next week and let him know that Donny's friend "Henry" in Missoula still wanted an elk. We parted ways. I had mixed emotions about Mike's planned trip; I wasn't enthusiastic that Mike was going in alone but was grateful I was staying home.

The following weekend I got a call from Mike. He was preparing to head north to Orofino. He'd been talking to Lube about Donny's so called friend in Missoula (who was really warden Gary Burke) known to Lube as "Henry." During the call Rex had told Mike that Jimmy and his brother Norman had taken a guy hunting from Washington and they'd killed a bull elk north of Pierce. Rex didn't seem to know much else about the incident, but Mike hoped to get more information during the pending trip. The news about this elk confirmed our theory; it didn't matter whether we were in Orofino or not—the Charbonneau boys were killing and selling wildlife.

I'd given Mike the para-cargo 'chute when I was in Boise. He said that Lube was excited to get it and had told him he was planning on using it as a shade cover over his campfire ring. Mike promised to try to give me a call from Orofino to let me know what was going on. I told him to pee on Snow's Rock for me.

Bear season had started and since the snow line in the Salmon River mountains was so high, the bear baiters could get to places where they normally would have been snowed out. I was torn between getting out to look for illegal bear baits and waiting for Mike to call. I was concerned that Mike might need investigative support and I wouldn't be available to run something down for him while he was up there alone. But wanting to stay home and wait for Mike to call was based mostly on emotional tug and not cognitive thought. Being undercover had been the most stressful work I had ever done. The entire time had been spent partnering with Mike and never alone, except my short fishing adventure with Mickey White and my journey to the church. Although Mike and I hadn't been able to verbally communicate with each other while we were with the bad guys, just being together helped with the tension.

Sitting on my butt waiting for the phone to ring seemed a bit too much like a seventeen-year-old girl waiting for an invitation to the prom. Cabin fever kicked in, and Ben and I hit the road looking for baits. In Idaho, baiting bears is legal but regulated. Most hunters follow the baiting rules, and others don't. There seems to be three kinds of hunters: Those that wouldn't break the law for anything, those that would break the law if opportunity presented, and those that planned to break the law before they ever got in their truck (or Gremlin).

The worst baits are what wardens call a "dirty bait." They usually consist of out-of-date food still in wrappers dumped in the woods. The worst dirty bait I ever worked was one that consisted of 1,235 candy suckers complete with their paper sticks. I knew there were that many because I'd picked them up and counted them at the bait site. When the case went to court and the bear hunter was sentenced, Judge Roos looked at me and communicated his displeasure about me picking up the mess. He was right; both of us would have preferred the violator clean the bait up as part of his sentence.

The other issue the baiting regulations address is safety. Bear baiters are not allowed to bait within 200 yards of a maintained trail or road. There are many non-bear hunters that don't see the humor in unknowingly walking into a bear's dining room.

Another method of bear hunting that is legal in Idaho is hound hunting. Houndsmen have a reputation for unscrupulous behavior, and it's been my experience that this is caused by some houndsmen that are extraordinarily unethical and unlawful. One popular hound hunting method for bears is *rigging*. Rigging is done with a hound chained on top of a dog box in the back of a pickup truck. The houndsman slowly drives the back roads until the dog scents a bear and audibly lights up.

Baits and hound hunting go hand in hand. The unethical houndsmen will place multiple illegal baits just out of site from the road where they want to rig a dog. The lawful houndsmen (and they are out there) will rig a road without baits—or maintain a legal bait well off the road and then walk their dogs into it.

Thus I wasn't bored. There was plenty of game warden work to keep me busy while "Henderson" was supposedly in Fairbanks getting tuned up to smokejump.

I got a call from warden Russ Kozacek. He'd gotten a tip from warden Lew Huddleston out of Idaho Falls. Huddleston had pinched a guy by the name of Eddie Beason with an illegal deer the previous fall and the judge had taken his hunting privileges away. Eddie happened to be a houndsman. Lew had received information that he was camped in nearby Panther Creek hunting bear with his hounds, or in warden-speak, "hunting while revoked." Russ had been working the information and had located his camp and chained hounds on the Panther Creek Road, but couldn't catch him hunting. Russ had found a nearby dirty bait that he felt belonged to Beason, but he couldn't prove it and was wanting to know whether I would go sit on the bait and to see if I could catch Beason with a hound on it. It wasn't a bad idea, but it might take several days and a fair amount of luck to make the case. I came up with another idea. "Henderson" might be benched in Clearwater County but that didn't mean he couldn't work some other short-term case locally on this lawbreaker. I had heard the Beason name before but didn't believe I had ever contacted him in uniform.

I took some dirty clothes out of my laundry basket and put them on. I pulled my .38 revolver out of my daypack, stuffed it inside my pants and covered it with my shirttail. We didn't have any information that Beason was dangerous but we didn't have any information that he wasn't, either. I took my old lever action .30-30

Winchester out of the gun safe and loaded the magazine leaving the chamber empty. I had inherited the carbine from my granddad Henderson, and hence it was a remarkable memento. Ben was well aware that something interesting was afoot. His ears were up and was wagging his tail in anticipation. I looked him in the eye and told him he would have to stay put. His long ears sagged in disbelief as he watched me walk out the door. I got in my personal truck, a faded tan '78 short-box, four-wheel drive Ford pickup, and headed for Panther Creek. Tony Henderson was reincarnated.

I found the illegal's camp on Panther Creek at the mouth of Blackbird Creek and drove by, trying not to rubberneck. A Dodge pickup truck was parked at the camp with a hound box in its bed. The license plate indicated it was from Mud Lake, the tiny little burg where Beason was from. There were a half-dozen hound dogs chained up, and a guy was out with a bucket watering the dogs. He looked ragged and the dogs looked as if they'd run a bear that morning. The guy had to be Eddie Beason.

I turned off the Panther Creek Road onto the Blackbird Road and drove up the canyon less than a rifle-shot and parked. I sat for a few minutes letting the dust settle. I took out my granddad's Winchester, stepped off the road and emptied the rifle into the hillside, making sure the brass casings ejected back onto the road. I reloaded pushing six fresh rounds into the magazine, levered one into the chamber, and lowered the hammer to half-cock. I sat and waited for fifteen minutes, and drove back down to Beason's camp. I pulled into the camp and jumped out of my truck. Beason stood and looked at me.

"I think I just wounded a bear and need to borrow or rent a couple of hounds if I can," I yelled.

I knew he wouldn't let me take his dogs, and I couldn't solicit him to break the law since any predisposition I had on him was borderline, but he paused and took the bait.

"I'll just go up there with you. My dogs'll find your bear," he chimed. "Was that you I heard shootin' up the creek just now?"

"Yeah, he's a big cinnamon. It's right up the road here!"

"Lemme get my boots on and I'll follow you up."

Eddie Beason quickly booted up, unchained three of his hounds, and loaded them into his wooden hound box in the bed of his truck. I drove up Blackbird Creek to where my shells were lying and got out with the Winchester. Beason pulled up, and I pointed up on the hill.

"I was standing right here, and the bear was over on the hill and he disappeared up in the trees."

Beason glanced down at the empty brass lying in the dust. He unloaded a black long-eared hound dog that looked like a cross between a Walker and a Plott.

"This is Trooper. If any hound can catch him, it's gonna be Troop. I'll put him out on the scent and turn the other two loose when he's got the trail."

He snapped a leash on the dog's collar and headed up the hill with Trooper pulling and me following with granddad's .30-30.

"You been doing any good with your dogs?" I asked.

"We chased one this morning, but he wouldn't tree."

Trooper did his best to find the missing scent. Beason worked the dog back and forth across the hill and finally turned back to me.

"Are you sure this is where he was?"

I pulled my badge wallet out of my back pocket and opened it up with my left hand exposing my badge and credentials.

"Tony Latham, Idaho Fish and Game. You're Eddie Beason, aren't you?"

His jaw dropped to speak, but his brain failed. He couldn't form any words, his shoulders slumped in resignation and he knew I had him.

"Look Eddie, this isn't the biggest problem in the world but I'm going to have to give you a ticket, so lets go on back to the truck and you can be on your way." I followed Eddie and Trooper back to the road. He produced his driver's license, and I directed him to stand in front of my truck so I could keep an eye on him while I filled out the citation from the driver's seat. I also filled out a seizure tag and receipt for evidence.

I stepped back out of the truck and explained the citation.

"The charge is 'pursue or attempt to pursue bear while license privileges are revoked.' It's a misdemeanor and you'll have to come back to Salmon for court."

"I just really like spring bear hunting with my dogs."

Then, I dropped the bomb and handed him the receipt for evidence.

"I'm seizing your dog; you'll get him back after the case has been adjudicated."

I reached over and took Trooper's leash and quickly put the dog up in my cab. Beason's face had turned dour; his shoulders were up and his eyebrows were down.

"Goddamn it, you're not taking my dog!"

"Chill out Eddie, you'll get him back. Relax." I eased into the driver's seat never turning my back on Beason and drove off.

On the way to town, Trooper was a fine companion and I felt a bit guilty for seizing him, he wasn't the violator. Eddie Beason wasn't going to be a big fan of mine and Bob Hammer probably wasn't going to give me a plaque for officer of the year over it but I had done my job. It was a solid case.

I took Trooper to the same kennel where I had been boarding Ben. Debbie, the owner, met me in the yard and asked what was going on with the hound. I explained to her that the dog was seized as evidence and the state would pay for the boarding. She frowned and gave me a disconcerted look, but she led Trooper into his temporary jail.

When I got home, Ben was happy I was back. He put his nose to my Levis and read his version of the case report. I unloaded the Winchester and put it in the gun safe, thinking about the Beason case. A year ago I would have hidden in the bushes for a few long days at the illegal bait hoping for Beason to show with a dog, but Mike Best and Gary Burke had given me another skill set: The covert option.

Chapter 18

Missoula Run

Mike finally called after being under for four days. He'd called from Grangeville just to tell me he was clear and then the following day he filled me in on what I had missed.

He'd met Lube at the Ponderosa restaurant and bought him dinner. Lube had told Mike about a bull elk that Jimmy and his brother Norman had gone out and killed the past week with a white man from Everett, Washington by the name of Rocky. They'd returned to the lodge and tried to call Burke in Montana to talk about the pending sale. Mike gave Lube the parachute, and he was elated with it and had plans to put it over his fire ring.

The next morning Norman Charbonneau showed up with his girlfriend Kathy. I'd asked Mike whether he'd seen any bullet scars on her head, but he laughed it off. He said he had no idea if she were the same woman that Norman had shot and he wasn't about to ask him. Norm had come to the lodge in hopes that the "man from Montana," as they were referring to him, still wanted an elk. Lube called Burke and they sealed the deal on the order and explained they'd have to go kill it. During the call he bragged to Burke that he moved wild game through his lodge by the tonnage and offered to sell him a piece of moose meat that weighed 38 pounds. Burke agreed to the moose at the ongoing $3 per pound price. Lube promised Burke to send it over with "Pate".

"Norm's a different man than his older brother," Mike said. "He's big and strong and not overweight but still drinks like a fish. He's got a car, and I get the idea that he does some part time work. I ran him for a driver's license, and he's got one but it's revoked right now over a DUI from this winter. His girlfriend is all wrinkled up from constant smoking; I don't think she said two words the whole time I was around her."

Later that morning Mike had gone with Jimmy and Norm and they had driven the Craigmont road hunting elk. Despite driving for most of the day, they didn't see any elk close enough to the road to shoot. They had seen a bear standing in the road that Jimmy had tried to kill, but it fortunately had gotten away.

The following morning at 4:00 a.m., Mike picked Norm and Jimmy up, and they headed past Pierce, beyond where Jimmy had killed the French Creek moose with us and out to Tamarack Ridge. The trip's purpose was to find an elk that they could kill and sell to the "man in Montana" for $3 a pound. At 8:15 they found a herd of elk and both Jimmy and Norm opened up. Jimmy was shooting his .243, and Norm was using a . 30-06. Jimmy killed one and Norm wounded another. The downed elk was close enough to the road to reach with Jimmy's rope and it was carrying an unborn calf. There was no effort to go after the wounded elk. They returned to the Crabtree with the elk just after noon. Lubinski called Burke when they got in and the decision was made to run it and the 38 pounds of moose meat the four hours to Missoula that afternoon.

Jimmy rode up front with Mike. For some reason that Mike didn't understand, Norm and his girlfriend Kathy wanted to tag along and got in the back with the elk. I had driven that winding highway along the Lochsa numerous times and I was happy it wasn't me in their place.

Mike said the trip to Missoula was uneventful except for the fact that Jimmy talked about his poaching. It was Mike's interpretation that Jimmy used the word to describe his trafficking activity and not the illegal killing of wildlife. Jimmy said he'd started doing it when he was eighteen and had recently sold a hind elk quarter to somebody who lived in the Hidden Village Trailer Court across from Orofino. He offered to guide Mike on what Jimmy called a trophy bull moose hunt in the fall for $150 a day and a $600 kill fee. It was a similar offer to what Tom had offered to me for a whitetail hunt, and Mike and I agreed that the rate was probably based on some kind of service they had provided in their past, but neither of us could understand why anybody would *want* to hunt with these guys—especially road hunt. What glimpses Mike and I had into Jimmy Charbonneau's life in the last few months led us to conclude that his sole source of income was the illegal selling of wildlife.

They met Burke in Missoula about 7:00 p.m. and Burke paid Jimmy $565 for the elk and the moose meat. They transferred the meat in a restaurant parking lot concealed behind a semi-trailer and then Burke bought them all dinner at Sizzlers. During the meal Jimmy said he'd split the money with Norm after he paid Lubinski off. Jimmy and Burke discussed the possibility of future orders, and Jimmy told him not to go through Lubinski but to call him direct and provided a phone number. Jimmy stated that the number was his father's. He also told Burke to use the code words; small potatoes for deer, red potatoes for elk, and black walnuts for moose meat.

They departed Missoula about 8:00 p.m. and Mike managed to get Jimmy to talk about the eagle feather trade on the way back. Jimmy said he shot eagles with his .243 and got $10 to $15 per feather, and he sold both the wing feathers and the tail feathers. He added that he and his brother sometimes made the feathers into tassels and fans that could bring between $400 and $500. And as Jimmy put it: It's legal to sell them unless you get caught." He also explained to Mike that if he got caught the tribe could take his hunting rights and tribal card.

Mike dropped the three passengers off in Orofino and got back to Lubinski's lodge at midnight. He'd logged a twenty-hour day and by any game warden's definition it was a long one.

The next morning Lubinski complained to Mike about Jimmy. He didn't think he'd ever see the money from the moose meat he'd sent to Missoula and would try to recruit another tribal member to launder his meat. Before Mike left, Rex sold him 150 pounds of frozen elk meat for $450.

Unfortunately, Mike had not been able to get Jimmy to talk about his other Montana customers on the trip. Mike and I both agreed that in a perfect trafficking investigation, you'd ensnare both the sellers and the buyers. We had numerous criminal charges on both Lubinski and Jimmy. We'd been able to put one count on Earl Lanolin for buying the fish stolen from the church, but he was the only buyer we had. Lube had given Mike a lead on an elk that had gone to a buyer in Washington but that was it for buyers. In hindsight, Mike's "Donny shtick" with wild game feeds was working great to nail the sellers, but it hadn't revealed their buyers. Mike decided to try to use his traveling salesman cover to facilitate Jimmy's deliveries, and hopefully get into his market.

On the Missoula trip, Mike had figured out that Jimmy's trailer was parked in front of his dad's house, and he'd gotten the house's phone number. He decided to start a dialogue with Jimmy over the phone and offer to deliver meat in association with Mike's claimed business travels. If his plan didn't work, we needed to start thinking about taking the case down. Burke had told us at the Harriman training that "the hardest decision to make during an undercover case was deciding when to take it down." When he'd brought it up, I really hadn't grasped the substance of it but I was starting to get it. Tom had offered to take me on an illegal whitetail hunt. Jimmy had offered an illegal moose hunt to Mike. It was obvious we could just continue breaking the law with this wild bunch, but in the end you could only squeeze so much juice out of an onion.

Chapter 19

Buzzguns

Mike began this secondary goal of the investigation by making a series of phone calls to Lube and Jimmy with the hopes of being asked to deliver contraband to customers as part of his business travels.

He'd make the call, write up a report about what was said and give a copy of the recording to the SIU office in Boise. The secretaries would transcribe the conversation. I'd get a copy and pick through it. What struck me the most about the conversations that he initiated wasn't the continual illegal killing of elk and moose but Mike's gift of gab. I felt sorry for who was doing the transcriptions. I don't think Mike ever made a covert call that didn't last a good twenty minutes. Most of the transcriptions were over twenty-five pages in length. Mike didn't focus on hunting or meat during these conversations but just began by asking an innocuous question such as, "what you been up to?" and take it from there.

A call to Lubinski in May revealed that he had continued to hunt closed season and hinted that it had been with tribal members. He didn't reveal names or location but admitted to killing an elk and a moose, referring to them as red potatoes and black walnuts. Mike called Jimmy's father's phone thinking he would leave a message, but Jimmy picked it up while watching a basketball game. During the thirty-minute conversation, Jimmy talked about salmon fishing and asked whether Mike could find him some two inch fishhooks for gaffing salmon and Mike promised to find some. Mike threw out that he would be making a business run in a couple of weeks and could help Jimmy out "if he needed anything hauled anywhere." He didn't bite.

A follow-up call to the Charbonneau number in June resulted in Norm answering. He said that he and a guy by the name of Andy had been out trying to kill bull elk. This was a curious piece of information since it made us speculate if they weren't involved in selling velvet elk antlers to the Asian medicinal trade—why else focus on bulls in the velvet? He complained of totaling his car when he hit an elk near Kamiah and that he had been drinking hard lately. In telling the story to Mike he expressed no remorse for killing the elk. Instead he was pissed at the elk for destroying his car.

By the end of June, it was clear that Plan B wouldn't get us into the buyers. Mike and I kicked things around and decided we needed to start moving towards the takedown, or raid phase, of the investigation. The raid would include search warrants and arrests at the Crabtree and probably Charbonneau's, along with interviews with other persons including Kristy Washer, Earl Lanolin, and Lube's kids in Wisconsin. All this would be done simultaneously, requiring numerous officers. It would take a lot of planning, and we needed to set a date. Roger discussed it with Snow and Kilgore, and they came up with a rough target of September 1st.

Mike and I were concerned with the Polaroid the sheriff had obtained of Lubinski with machine guns. Snow had discussed the issue with Sheriff Albers. Albers believed it would be prudent to use the county SWAT team to secure the lodge and safely arrest Lubinski in the event that he had a machine gun at hand. Along this same line Mike decided that we needed to make a trip to the Crabtree to attempt to gain additional information on the type of weapons Lubinski had and where they might be hidden. True to form, Mike came up with a plan. He'd borrowed a British Sten gun from the Ada County Sheriff's Department to use as a "flash" with Lubinski.

He prepped Lubinski with a phone call, telling him I had been moved from Fairbanks to Boise due to an increase in fire activity and that I was ready to take some time off. Mike also included a cover story about dickering on a machine gun, complaining that he couldn't find a place to shoot it in California, and that he wanted to bring it up to Orofino. Rex didn't seem to blink about the machine gun.

It was time to suit up again, and get back in role. I really wouldn't need any special gear on this trip, just a duffle bag of clothing and my daypack with its hidden revolver. I went through my clothing and toilet bag looking for any tell that would betray us. I found a stack of evidence tags in my daypack. Other than that, everything looked clean. I dropped Ben off at the kennel, withdrew a couple hundred bucks from the bank and headed to McCall.

Mike showed me the Sten gun. It was a pitted, course-looking subgun that was perfect for what we needed it to do. He'd also purchased several boxes of 9mm rounds to assist with the flash.

"By the way," Mike said, "You won't be fishing with your buddy Mickey White anymore."

"What do you mean?" I asked.

"His girlfriend tried to leave him. He shot her in the face, killed her dead. She had a thirteen-year old kid he tried to kill, also. He's charged with first degree."

"You're kidding me. Who the hell told you that?" I asked.

"Snow."

I sat in Mike's truck staring out the window, thinking about the time I had spent with Mickey and Judy and letting this news sink into my bones. Another layer of my naiveté had been ripped away.

The trip north from McCall was becoming rote. Much of the green that had existed in late March had dried up. The main Clearwater was glass clear. Even with the news about Mickey, for some strange reason, it felt good to be back. We fueled up in Orofino about 6:00 p.m., drove by the hatchery, passed the Woodlot and up the Ahsahka Grade. I must have been back in role because I had a notion to pee on Snow's Rock.

Mike pulled into the Crabtree's driveway. I could see that Rex had rigged the white parachute canopy over the fire pit, using a lodgepole in its center and staking out the lines. Lubinski was sitting in the shade of the lodge on a dilapidated lawn chair drinking a beer. His tooth-missing smile lit up his face when he saw us drive in. He had on his trademark black jeans and chain wallet, topped off with a grungy, black, sleeveless t-shirt. His brown hair was overdue for a barber. I stepped out of the truck's air-conditioned climate and was hit by the heat of summer. Rex opened up two more chairs that needed to make a one way dump-run, and we sat down.

"You guys bring up that buzzgun?" he quizzed.

"Yeah, we did," I answered. "I've never shot one."

Mike pulled the Sten out of his rig, pulled the gun's bolt back and pulled the trigger, letting the bolt slam on its empty chamber. Rex registered about as much interest in it as if it were a kid's .22 rifle. His lack of inquisitiveness was unexpected.

"You can make a pretty good silencer for them with a Briggs and Stratton muffler," Rex said.

"You always amaze me with your know-how," Mike replied.

"There's a guy in town that's got a couple of machine guns still in Cosmoline grease he's trying to sell," Rex threw out.

I was struck with the fact that Rex was a well-stocked warehouse of crime. There wasn't much going on that he wasn't associated with. "What do they shoot?" I asked, "I probably couldn't even afford to feed one."

"Well," Rex answered. "I don't know exactly what they are, but I can find out if you're interested."

"I am," I asserted. "But I'd have to figure out what they'd cost to shoot."

We left the heat and walked into the lodge past the pond-smelling hot tub. The inside hadn't changed. Rex's hat with the eagle feather was hung on the wall where it had been when we'd left. The photo album containing the pictures of his two sons and illegal elk was still on the bookshelf, and a half-rack of Keystones was stacked in the refrigerator. Rex handed a couple of beers to us with grease-stained hands and proceeded to cook us up a meal of fried deer steaks. His lack of cleanliness around the kitchen hadn't reversed itself during the course of summer. In the middle of the meal, I heard the rumble of the Gremlin.

"That'll be Kristy," Rex volunteered.

She came through the door with another guy and a gal laughing at a joke we hadn't heard, and I suspected hadn't been told.

"This is Bill and Olivia," Rex offered, "They're staying up here and are helping me out."

The couple looked like long lost souls from Woodstock. All three had bloodshot glassy eyes and smelled of fresh weed smoke. Bill grabbed two beers from the refrigerator and sat down with Olivia in the living room. Kristy sat down at the table still giggling.

"You guys going huntin'?" She asked.

"Who knows?" I answered. "We mainly just came up to see our bud here, besides I needed to get out of Boise for a few days."

Rex asked me about smokejumping, so I repeated some jump stories I'd heard over the years, claiming they were mine. I talked about the coming fire season and how it was setting itself up to be a good one. "Henderson" was in his deceitful prime. "Pate" had a spark in his eyes enjoying my dishonesty.

The following morning, Rex was the only one up. Mike suggested the three of us go down to the Ponderosa for breakfast. I assumed Rex hadn't slept in his clothes, but he was wearing the same garb as the previous night. The three of us slid onto the front seat of Mike's pickup with Rex and his halitosis in the middle.

The Ponderosa was winding down from its morning rush. As the waitress took our orders I recognized her as the same one that had served us the night Jimmy had assaulted Trudy. The food was tasty and the coffee was fresh.

"Norm and I got a cow a couple weeks ago," Rex bragged. "He shot it with his thirty-ought-six. We went out two days ago and got a spike buck in Washington Creek. He shot the damn thing with his ought-six even though I had my twenty-two; he blew the shit out of it. I've got it hanging out behind the lodge."

"Was that what we had for dinner?" Mike asked.

"Yep," Rex smirked.

Mike picked up the bill, and we drove over to Jimmy's. We found him in his father's house. His camp trailer was connected to it with an electrical cord. He was unkempt and alone; somehow he'd managed to gain weight in our absence. I wondered if he'd been forced onto a solid food diet in jail. He was sullen and explained he had been arrested by the FBI.

"It's over that thing with the girl," he explained. "There's some guy supposed to be showing up to put some kinda bracelet on my ankle so I can't sneak off."

256

"I can't have no guns anymore either," he lamented. "I'm just gonna keep 'em at my sister's so I can get them when I need 'em."

We small talked for a bit, said *adios*, and got back in Mike's rig.

"Jesus," Rex declared. "If I knew I was gonna be arrested, I'd run."

"Where would you go?" I asked.

"I don't know."

When we got back to the lodge Olivia and Kristy were smoking at the dining room table. I heard Kristy mumble something about forging her rent verification for welfare.

The smoke was thick in the dining room, so Mike and I sat down in the living room with Bill.

"You're helping Rex run this place?" Mike asked.

"Yeah, we answer the phone, Olivia does some cleaning," Bill replied. "I helped butcher half of that deer the other day too."

"The one he'n Norm got?" I asked.

"Yeah, the spike. I went out last winter and got a couple of 'em for myself."

I had grown so used to hearing of lawlessness that this information didn't surprise me, but now we'd have to figure out his last name. Rex had said that half of the deer was still hanging out back and if we got a look-see at it we'd have enough to charge Bill with "principal to unlawful possession." Not a strong case, but strong enough to give him a ticket.

Lubinski showed us a 6X scope he had installed on his .22 rifle. He said he had shot it once but wanted to make sure it was sighted in. He grabbed a hand full of shells from a coffee mug on the bookshelf and dumped them in his shirt pocket. He fished an empty beer can from the trash and walked out the front door with Mike and me following. As soon as we got outside Rex saw a mourning dove perched on a power line next to his driveway and levered a round into the chamber. He dropped the beer can and took an offhand shot at the dove, dropping it in a flutter of feathers.

"Well, I guess it's right on," he laughed. He made no effort to retrieve the bird. It was two more counts; "take closed season and wasteful destruction." I made a mental note to try to retrieve the dead dove.

The sun sank below the ridge, and the heat slackened with the shade. Mike insisted we go shoot the Sten. The three of us loaded up in Mike's truck. Rex had us turn right at the end of his driveway. We passed Gardiner's Taxidermy and got up into the timber.

"Turn in here," Rex instructed. "I cut poles in here sometimes, and nobody's ever bothered me."

The place was riddled with two-rut roads and thinned over timber. He was right; it was an out-of-the-way place, a good spot to rattle the woods with noise. Mike got out a cardboard box of 9mm ammunition from behind his seat and set it and the Sten down on the truck's tailgate. While Mike loaded the gun's 32-round magazine, I looked the weapon over. It was crude. At one time, it had been painted but most of it had worn off. The receiver was made from a piece of pipe about two inches in diameter. The barrel was about eight inches long, and it had an open steel butt stock. The bolt had a fixed firing pin on its face. The coiled mainspring behind the bolt appeared as if it belonged in a washing machine. It looked like a biker's gun.

Mike picked up the weapon and inserted the magazine into its port on the left side of the receiver just behind the barrel, pointed it at the empty milk jug that Rex had thrown out and hissed half a magazine off with three quick bursts. I took the weapon and finished it off with a final burst. You held the magazine with your left hand, cradled the metal stock with your right and pulled the trigger at gut level to fire the weapon. The bolt would ram forward, pull a round off the magazine and slam fire when the cartridge smacked into the chamber. The gun would continue to fire until the trigger was let off. It took no effort to hit the milk jug with six to ten round bursts from thirty feet. It was a fun little gun to shoot, and each time I emptied a magazine, I'd laugh spontaneously. Oddly Rex had no interest in shooting the weapon. Mike and I interpreted his lack of curiosity as "been there, done that." We were hoping to get a reaction something like, "That's nothing—let me show you what I've got at home," but it didn't happen.

After burning up several hundred rounds we headed back down to the lodge. Rex talked about the guy in Orofino with the machine guns, mentioned his name was Cal, and promised to look into it for me. Olivia cooked us a meal of barbecued venison steak and fried potatoes. I was relieved to see her wash her hands. We ate outside under the parachute canopy with a campfire Rex had lit. Mike asked him whether the steaks were from the deer that he and Norm had killed, and he confirmed that it was. Kristy came out with a cigarette hanging off her lip and sat down with us. Rex talked about his continuing efforts to turn the lodge into a whorehouse. Kristy failed to complain about the idea. It was an unorthodox but enjoyable summer evening at the Crabtree.

The following morning Rex suggested we fish the reservoir in his boat. The hull didn't have a valid Idaho boat registration on it, so Rex took a felt marker and wrote NPT 208 on it and explained it was Jimmy's tribal number. If we got checked he'd claim he had borrowed the boat from Jimmy. We hitched the boat trailer to his Dodge. Lube threw in some cheap fishing poles, a tackle box and a cooler full of Keystone. Rex drove down the grade and turned up the North Fork. A half mile past the dam we pulled into a developed site with a boat ramp and parking lot. Mike and I got out and Lube backed the trailer into the water with me holding the bowline. Lubinski parked the truck and we loaded up into the boat. The motor started without a hitch. Rex idled the boat into deeper water and throttled up. The engine revved up and down. The hull wallowed and couldn't quite get up on plane. Rex idled down, turned the motor off, and gave me a quizzical look.

"This engine's supposedly got thirty hours on it."

He raised the prop and looked it over without finding any seaweed. He lowered it down again and restarted it. We motored off on half plane with me wondering if we were going to make it back to the dock. Mike gave me a knowing glance pondering the same question. About a quarter mile from the ramp, Rex pulled into a small bay, rigged three rods and we started trolling. He went back and forth in the bay complaining about the Kokanee and drinking beer. He picked Mike's brain again for information on how much meat Donny would need for the fall feed and Mike ad-libbed. Finally after two beers, Lube gave up and chugged back to the dock.

We managed to get the boat loaded on the trailer. Rex pulled up next to the kiosk at the site's exit. There was a roll of plasticized reservoir maps padlocked onto a welded steel pipe. The maps showed campsite locations around the reservoir that the Corp of Engineers had developed. The maps looked expensive. Rex took a furtive look around, quickly rolled off an armful, and ripped the pile off its roll. "I'm gonna use 'em for placemats at the lodge," he explained while stashing the maps behind his seat.

We drove back down and unhitched the boat behind the lodge.

"Where's this spike buck you and Norm got?" Mike asked. "I wanna see the horns."

Rex showed us into a rundown wooden outbuilding and we were greeted by blowflies. Hanging inside the shed was the yearling buck minus the hindquarters. The animal had been skinned up to its head and hung by a rope around the base of its antlers. The deer's tongue was dangling out of the side of its mouth, and its eyes had shrunken back into their sockets. A handful of maggots was squirming in the exit hole where Norm's bullet had burst out the animal's shoulder.

"Shit," Rex exclaimed. "I'm probably going to have to dump this on my bone pile up where we shot your gun. Bill and I are gonna move a walk-in cooler up here next week; that'll keep this from happening again."

Mike and I walked back to the lodge. We went to our room, lying down on our beds as an excuse to get away from Lube. I whispered to Mike about needing to figure out Bill's last name.

"It's Magnum, Bill Magnum—there's a stack of his mail down there," he whispered back.

I tried to sleep, but it wouldn't happen, and I wished I'd brought a book. After a bit, I heard a car roll in, followed by Norm's voice. Mike looked at me, shrugged, and we walked down stairs to the main floor.

Norm was sitting down with an Indian woman with long black hair. Both were drinking blue Keystones. He and Lube were laughing. I could smell chicken cooking in the kitchen, and I looked over and saw Bill and Olivia preparing dinner.

"Hey, Norm how you doing, bud?" Mike asked. "You get a new car or something?"

"Yeah, I bought a Pinto. It ain't as good as the one that elk destroyed, but it'll get me around," he chuckled. "This is Kathy, my girlfriend," he announced to me.

We ate dinner. When we were done, Kathy was sloshed and speaking for a change. She was talking about a night out at the Jet Club. "I was drinking rum and that stuff always makes me crazy," she explained. "Jimmy was there, and I was a real bitch to him."

"Don't call yourself a bitch, goddamn it," Norm spat at her and stood up. And then, he sucker punched her in the face with his big fist and stormed outside. I walked over to the window and watched him drive off in the Pinto. I glanced back at Kathy. She was holding her face with both hands but I couldn't see any blood. *At least he hadn't broken her nose,* I thought. Olivia was kneeling beside her with both arms wrapped around her like a sister. It was a bad deal and I was damn glad he'd left.

The next morning Mike and I were ready to hit the road and get out of Lubinski's life. We drank coffee and turned down his offer of breakfast. I claimed I needed to check into the fire center before dark. I asked Rex to find out more about the machine guns and to let Pate know what he found out. Mike gave Rex a check for the board and room, and we took off.

Chapter 20

Imminent Retribution

Compared to the March trip, this last one had been a blink—but it felt too long. I was getting tired of Lube and his pals. It would be good to turn the corner on this case and take it down.

The Sten hadn't smoked out any of Rex's arsenal but in my gut it had reinforced our theory that he had automatic weapons. It'd also brought out Rex's knowledge of a guy selling automatic weapons that were probably stolen from the military. On the way home, I'd asked Mike if he thought we needed to go after the subguns. He got wound up and glanced at me as though I was missing something.

"Hell yes, we need to go after 'em," he answered. "The only felony we've gotten on Lube right now is the burglary and I'm not sure Swain will make that one stick. The wildlife charges on him are misdemeanors. If he wants to help us buy a machine gun, let's let him do it. He might end up doing some time and he damn sure won't be able to possess firearms anymore—that would crimp his poaching."

"I agree, but how are you gonna sell the idea to Roger?" I asked.

"I don't have to," Mike smiled. "I'll throw it at Squires, and he'll tell us to go after the damn guns. That'll be that."

Mike was right. The department wouldn't support our trying to buy a machine gun, but his boss was smart enough to avoid bucking a prosecutor who wanted it pursued. However, it would be up to Lubinski now to grease the skids on the deal. Since it appeared that he was too inept to reach his goal of luring prostitutes to the lodge, Mike and I were doubtful he could really pull it together on getting us an illegal buzzgun.

Mike called me up to kick around some thoughts he was having on the raid. There was no doubt we needed to arrest Lube. He'd already talked about going on the lam. An early morning arrest at the lodge would ensure he wouldn't escape. The problem that Mike had pondered was named Norm Charbonneau. Jimmy wasn't an issue since he was already under house arrest by the FBI. Even if he ran, we were confident that the Bureau would haul his butt back. Norm's situation was different. First of all he was dangerous. He'd tried to kill one person and the battery he'd committed in our presence affirmed his volatility. The one good charge we had on him was trafficking in Montana. Serving state warrants on tribal members on the reservation wasn't in the cards because of their sovereignty. To solve these challenges, Mike believed we should try to put together a buy-bust operation targeting Norm in Missoula on raid day.

The other issue we discussed was how to freshen up the evidence we wanted to seize at the lodge with a warrant. Evidence listed on a search warrant can't include anything that has become stale. The concept of "fresh" versus "stale" within the search warrant world is a bit vague. Even without seizing anything from Lubinski we had a tight case against him. However, there were several items that had significant evidentiary value that would enhance the case against him and others, and a warrant might open the door to other charges. What we really hoped to get were his bolt cutters, his .22 rifle, the photo album, moose hair in the Gremlin, and the eagle feather. Right now, the *probable cause* that these items were still at the lodge was stale. We'd need to freshen it up with one last visit to the Crabtree and with luck, buy a machine gun with Lube's help.

Two weeks after we'd returned from the Clearwater, Rex called Mike, and bragged that he and Norm had killed four bull elk. Mike quizzed him on how they were storing the meat in the August heat.

"We've already moved some of them," Rex answered. "The rest we've got hanging in our cooler, but it's been giving us some fits."

Mike and I both agreed that he'd meant that they had "sold" the meat when he used the term "moved." Rex had asked Mike what the amount of meat Donny was anticipating needing for the fall game feed. When he'd asked this, he used the word "tonnage." In order to discourage more killing, Mike told him the feed had been postponed and wouldn't happen until October. Rex also said he had not been able to get hold of Cal, the guy with the machine guns, but would keep trying.

Burke called Jimmy to order another elk to start the Missoula buy-bust in motion. As expected, Jimmy explained that Burke would have to deal with Norm since he had "gotten in a little trouble." Burke began a dialogue with Norm and of course the deal began to come together. Burke specified frozen meat knowing they had already killed the four bulls and didn't want to cause another elk to die.

Mike and I started planning the raid. The task intimidated me. We would need the search warrant served on the lodge, Lube arrested and transported to jail. Jimmy Charbonneau would be interviewed and served with formal complaints. Other interview subjects included Newt Isaac, Kristy Washer, Bill and Olivia Magnum, Tom Charbonneau, and Earl Lanolin. Wisconsin wardens would hit the Lubinski boys' houses, and Montana would arrest Norm in Missoula assuming Venus and Mars aligned. And all this would have to go down in one day. I was baffled.

"Relax," Mike explained. "Actually, it's easy to put together a plan for this. Just begin by listing each objective and figure out how many officers it'll take. Albers' SWAT team will secure the lodge and arrest Lubinski. We'll need, what? Four conservation officers to search the lodge? Probably a female officer or two to help handle Kristy and Olivia. We oughta have at least three, maybe four officers interview Jimmy—two for the interview and two for security. Two guys can cover Tom, and we'll need two good interviewers to question Lubinski in jail. Wisconsin can come up with four officers to hit the boys back there. Montana can arrest Norm in Missoula. *No problemo, amigo.*"

Mike was right; his experience from his days with the Secret Service was showing through. It was just a matter of articulation. Having been on other raids I was aware that Mike and I would also need to put together raid packets for each team that outlined their objectives. The packets would include driver's license photos of each person they were assigned to contact, where they might be found, background on what crimes they had been involved in, what we wanted them to accomplish, and any special risk we believe existed. And that meant a lot of paper work for Mike and me.

Roger Jones and Dwight Kilgore were handling other details that needed to be worked out. They'd have to determine where they would get the fourteen Idaho officers and where to brief them. Dwight decided the Ahsahka hatchery would be the perfect facility from which to brief and coordinate the actual raid. The briefing would be conducted the night before the raid. The officers driving in would only be initially told that they would be staying in Lewiston on the night of September 2nd and would be involved in enforcement operations the following day. The raid officers would also have to be briefed collectively so they would understand what the other teams were doing and would have a chance to ask questions.

Burke would handle the raid prep from the Montana side. Wisconsin Department of Natural Resources would distribute their two raid packets the same night as the Idaho briefing.

Mike and I kicked around the problem of obtaining the arrest and search warrants. There was no question that we had enough *probable cause*. The problem was that one or both of us would have to appear before a judge in the Orofino courthouse to get them. In kicking it around, Mike suggested that we come up with a ruse that would put me somewhere away from the Crabtree the day before the raid and that Lee Squires and I would hammer out the affidavits and take them before the judge. Mike would take Norm to Missoula the next morning and sometime after that, Albers' SWAT team would hit the lodge. It would take close to thirty officers and four agencies in three states to pull off.

Mike set the stage by contacting Lubinski to let him know I was taking some time off and that we wanted to come up. Mike lied to him and told him about a fire meeting I'd have to attend in Moscow on the 2nd to cover my warrant meeting with Squires. Rex bragged about a moose he'd killed with Norman. He also brought up the meat deal between Norm and the "man in Montana" and Mike volunteered to drive Norm and the meat to Missoula.

This was our last undercover run. I can't say I was relaxed about it. The part that bothered me the most was that by the evening of September 2nd, there would be about thirty officers in the loop, plus the judge and court clerk. Two of the officers were going to be BIA tribal cops. But, the kicker was that Mike and I would be staying at the Crabtree that night. The tribal cops were going to be involved in facilitating interviews of tribal members on the reservation. It was the perfect storm for a lethal leak.

For the last time, I took Ben to the kennel and headed to McCall. This trip would be different from past trips, in that Mike and I needed separate vehicles. I was driving the Salmon Region's unmarked Bronco. Needless to say, the Bronco got a cleaning and it didn't involve looking for dirt.

Mike and I rendezvoused at the McCall Hatchery. We drove north on Highway 55 following the Little Salmon River into Riggins, crossed the main Salmon at Time-Zone Bridge, through the burg of Whitebird and up the grade to Grangeville. This would be the eleventh journey over this same route since January. It was highly diverse country—classic central Idaho.

We both gassed up in Orofino at the Texaco station and headed for the Crabtree. We caravanned into the lodge. A canvas Indian teepee had been erected beyond the parachute canopy. Norm Charbonneau's dirty orange Pinto was parked out front along with Bill Magnum's white Econoline van. Rex's showpiece Gremlin was wedged between them. The place was hopping.

Braless Kristy greeted us at the door smoking a cigarette and drinking a beer. Inside Rex and Olivia were cooking up dinner. Kathy and Norm were sitting on the couch drinking beer together, and it looked as if they'd kissed and made up.

Rex brought us a couple of Keystones and sat down with us. He was enthusiastic to have us back. "I got a bear bait going up above here and have a big bastard hitting it. It's up there where we went shooting."

"What you using for bait?" I asked.

"Bones and scraps from the elk plus a couple of whole ones we lost to flies. We oughta go up there tonight with the spotlight and get a piece of him."

"Have you seen him yet?"

"No, I think he's just coming in at night. All's I seen is his tracks, that's why I know he's big—plus he's eating like a hog."

"Well maybe it's just a little bear with big feet," I poked.

We sat down, and Olivia served us a moose roast dinner. It was a civil meal since Kathy had apparently learned her lesson and didn't refer to herself as a "bitch." After dinner, we migrated outside into the hot summer evening and drank beer under the parachute. Despite the temperature, Rex started a fire in the pit. The smoke kept swirling around causing all of us to squint. I leaned forward in the chair seeking some cleaner air while sipping on my beer and turned to Bill Magnum.

"You and Olivia from Orofino?"

"Naw, we moved from Seattle a year ago."

"I like this neck of the woods," I replied. "Rex and the Charbonneau boys have been good to Pate and me. I might just have to move up here. Hailey gets a lot of snow and I like this steelhead fishing here. What brought you guys here anyway?"

"I was selling a lot of dope and getting high too much. We both needed to quit. I was an undercover narc agent for King County. Hell, I was smoking crack while wearing a wire. It was some spooky shit, man."

"Jeez, I can't even imagine," I told him and drank a swig of my blue-canned grog.

Magnum's story was a lie. I didn't doubt he had been a user, and he'd probably sold. The part that was pure bull was his alluding that he'd been an undercover cop. What I suspected was that he had been caught holding some dope, or had sold some to an undercover and they'd put him in a twist and used him for a controlled buy or two. He may have even huffed on a pipe and compromised a case. I'd bet that the real reason for his move to the Clearwater was to run from the dopers he'd snitched on. I didn't miss the irony of his undercover yarn.

When it got dark, Rex suggested we run up the hill in Mike's truck and check his bear bait out. I liked the idea of getting away from the rest of the group and the hot smoky fire. I jumped in the middle. Rex grabbed his . 30-06 and his spotlight and slid onto seat next to me with a half six-pack of Keystone placed on the dash. We drove up past Gardiner's taxidermy and turned off on the same road where we'd shot the Sten gun. Rex had his window down and the warm summer air rolled into the cab. It was good to get away from the party smoke. Mike slowly eased his rig down the two-track and Rex lit up the timber with his spotlight. An open Keystone was trapped in his crotch, and his left hand held his rifle barrel up with the butt on the floor. *Some kind of bear hunt this is,* I thought.

Returning to the spot we'd shot the Sten at was a perfect excuse to segue to the machine gun question. "So," I said, "You get a chance to talk that guy about the buzzgun, Rex?"

"No, I've called him and left messages, but he won't call me back. I'm thinking that what he has shoots that . 30 Carbine round though."

"That's good," I said. "That sounds like it's something I could afford to shoot. I think you can still buy it surplus, can't you?"

"Yeah," he answered. "I think some buddies of mine do. I'll give the guy another call in the morning."

At least that gave us a clue on what the guns were. The army had used the M1 Carbine during World War II and the select fire version was called the M2. There was very little chance that the weapons were legally possessed. Besides, I hadn't known Rex's shadow to fall on anything legitimate.

Rex continued working the light in the area without finding the bear. I wasn't disappointed. Bear season wouldn't open until the following day. It was also illegal to spotlight for bears. So we had the elements to charge him for both. We'd also need to send a couple of wardens up to this location on raid day since it was illegal to use wild game parts to bait bear.

We returned to the lodge. Norm's Pinto was gone, along with Magnum's van. The place was empty. Rex believed the crew must have headed for the Jet Club. I took another beer from the refrigerator and retrieved Rex's photo album off the shelf and sat down looking as through I was really interested. Near the end, I found the photo of his two sons with the dead elk in Rex's pickup. It was Monday, August 31st—two days before the raid. The clock was ticking, and I could feel its beat.

The following morning Olivia had coffee going. She confirmed that they had all gone to the bars and had closed down the Jet Club. Everybody else would probably sleep in. She rustled up some grub consisting of

ground meat and eggs, and we sat down and ate with
Rex.

I didn't even bother to ask what the meat was. He
suggested we head up to Isabella Creek later after
breakfast and fish for Kokanee. He explained that the
fish had moved out of the reservoir and would be
spawning in the creek.

The phone rang, and he got up to answer it.
"Crabtree...yeah, this is Rex...how you been Henry? ...
No, Norm's asleep but he's planning on heading your
way with the red potatoes on Thursday...it's all frozen
and ready to go... yeah, I'll have Norm give you a call."

Rex topped his coffee off and sat down simpering.
"That was the man from Montana. Norm's gonna take a
load of frozen meat over this week."

"How the hell is he going to get a bunch of coolers in
that frigging Pinto?" Mike asked. "We should just run up
there in my truck."

Lube nodded. "Talk to Norm about it."

The crew slowly wandered down from their rooms.
Kristy came down wearing her pink sweat pants and an
oversized black t-shirt that I suspected was Rex's. Norm
had on his ragged jeans and an old paint-specked t-shirt
with cutoff sleeves. Bill didn't show.

The phone rang again and Rex picked it up.
"Crabtree... Yeah, this is Rex... no... look, I know these
guys, we been doing all sorts of shit..." He hung up and
looked off balance. He turned to Mike and me. "The guy
with the guns doesn't want to deal."

"Damn Rex," Mike exclaimed, "What kind of
gunrunner are you?"

"Shit," Rex answered. "The guy's being paranoid. I don't know what to tell yous guys."

Lubinski had just unknowingly dealt himself out of serious trouble, more consequential than killing gravid wildlife as far as the law was concerned. The machine gun issue would have to be addressed during Lube's interview after he was arrested.

Mike suggested we visit Jimmy on the way out of town. Rex got things moving and we loaded up Mike's rig. Norm got in front with Mike and Rex, and I took our places in the back with some cheap fishing poles that must have come from a garage sale. I had my daypack with its hidden .38. Norm had a scoped rifle up front and Rex had his .22 rifle with him. I mentally scratched his rifle off my list of items I needed to freshen for the warrant.

We stopped at Jimmy's trailer and found him inside his father's house. An old Indian with graying hair looked in from the kitchen and I assumed it was Jimmy's father. Jimmy lowered his bulk into a well-used couch and showed us his electronic ankle bracelet. I asked how it worked, and he explained it was somehow connected to the telephone. He told us his next court hearing would be in October, and his attorney thought he could get him off, based on a lack of Miranda warning along with no physical evidence of a rape when the girl had been taken to the hospital. I knew enough about the Justice Department to know that the likelihood of Hampton failing to read him his rights was about as likely as a snowstorm hitting the Clearwater that afternoon. I was also aware that Hampton would be providing Jimmy's attorney with a copy of our report next week.

The device was harnessed to Jimmy's ankle with a Kevlar band. He had a well-worn broken hammer handle that he'd crammed inside the device's strap and was working it back and forth. It looked as if he had made some progress, but I couldn't believe his efforts would work.

"If I get this damn thing off me I'm going to put it on dad and head for the rez in Colville," he declared.

"You get that thing off by Thursday you can ride up to Missoula with us," Mike offered.

"That gives me something to look forward to," he said and gave the hammer handle a pull.

On the way out to the truck, Norm yelled across the street at an Indian in his twenties who was sitting on a porch watching us.

"Hey, Clinton! We're going to Isabella Creek; you wanna go?"

"Yeah let me grab some stuff."

Norm and Mike loaded up front. Rex and I loaded in the back with Clinton crawling over the tailgate behind us. As soon as we were moving, Clinton picked up an empty Keystone can, bent it into a rough bowl shape and made a series of small pinpricks into it using a knife he'd pulled out his jeans. He pulled a baggie of marijuana out of his shirt pocket, sprinkled some of it into the can's bowl around the pricks and brought it to his mouth. He pulled a Bic lighter out of his shirt pocket and fired it up and brought the flame down to the pot. He took a deep drag on the apparatus, held the smoke in and then exhaled it into our space.

"This is some shitty fucking Mexican weed," he bitched.

I was ready to decline an offer from his pipe, but he failed to pass it off. I was glad the side windows of the canopy were pulled open, but the smoke still hung with us.

We drove out up through Orofino, through Grangemont, and into the big cedar country of the upper North Fork. The takedown clock wasn't ticking fast enough.

Clinton looked at me and glowered. "Fuckin' Europeans have ruined this country," he scowled.

I didn't answer. He'd made it clear he didn't like white people. I didn't like him either, but I kept my mouth shut. We crossed over the North Fork and finally made it out to Isabella Creek. Mike pulled over, and we unloaded. Norm and Clinton walked over to a log forty yards away and sat down. Clinton loaded his beer can pipe again, lit it with a big inhale and handed it to Norm.

Rex rigged up a couple of fishing poles with treble-hooked spoons and glanced at me shaking his head and smiled. "He's a big drug dealer with the Indians. I don't think he likes us."

Rex picked up both poles and handed me one. I followed him over to the creek. There was a deep clear pool with several spawning red Kokanee in the bottom. Rex cast the spoon in and started jerking the rod. He snagged a hump-backed male near the fish's dorsal fin; it broached and then was off. The ruckus scattered the school. Rex studied the pool for a bit looking for another target and then turned to me, "I'll show you how we fish for pike in Wisconsin."

He retrieved his rifle from the back of Mike's rig, and I followed him up the creek. We soon found another pool with fish. He snuck up to them, aimed into the water and fired. A stunned fish rolled over on its side and the current washed it over the gravel. Rex made no attempt to retrieve the fish. It was killing for sport.

"You wouldn't believe how many sacks of pike I've gotten back home this way."

"Actually," I declared, "I think I would."

After an hour of juvenile delinquency, we loaded up with Norm and Rex whining about the lack of beer. During the drive, back to 'Fino Clinton lit up his pipe again and exhaled his smoke into the silent truck canopy. I was happy to see him crawl over the tailgate when we got to the Charbonneau 'hood.

At the lodge, we pulled in next to Rex's teepee. I noticed a set of two-point elk antlers joined by a skullcap leaning on the lodge that I hadn't seen before and turned to Rex. "Where'd this bull come from?" I asked.

"It's that one that Norm and I got last month. I finished it off with my twenty-two."

It had been eight months since Mike and I had started this case, and I couldn't count how many animals that had died on our watch. Retribution was overdue.

Chapter 21

D-Day

The next morning I got up and put on a clean shirt before anyone else was moving and headed into Orofino. I grabbed coffee and a sweet roll "to go" at the Ponderosa. Rex believed I was headed to Moscow for a fire meeting, but instead I had a meeting with Lee Squires to write up the applications for search and arrest warrants.

I pulled behind the prosecutor's office and parked the Bronco as discreetly as possible. Squires met me at the back door. I followed him in, sat down in front of his hardwood desk and unloaded on him. I told him that the only people that I had met in the area that had any redeeming social value were Bill Snow, John Swain, and himself—I didn't understand how anybody could live in 'Fino. He frowned at my comment but sat listening and nodding. It was about all I could really expect since, what I had said was insulting. The constant and rampant sociopathic behavior of Jimmy, Rex, and all their pals and relatives had gotten under my skin.

Lee paused with his elbows on his desk and his palms open with his fingers touching each other. "I think if you lived here and saw this place from a different angle you'd see that it's full of fine people. I think you've been down in the gutter too long."

I was sure he was right, at least about me being in the gutter.

We got down to business. Lee had the case reports sprawled out and had been working on the search warrant affidavit. The affidavit for a search warrant is the written application for the actual warrant that the judge reviews to determine if there is cause for its issuance. Affidavits have four mandatory parts. The first is the officer's experience and training. Judges rely on this section to understand who the *affiant* is and what his or her knowledge is. Anything listed in the affidavit that requires special skills needs to be reflected in the affidavit under this first section. In this affidavit, I needed to be able to articulate how I had obtained knowledge that the eagle feather was truly from an eagle. Lee asked me about it, and I explained that I had collected several dead eagles along the highway and had been trained by a U.S. Fish and Wildlife agent in eagle feather identification. He added my eagle experience to the affidavit.

The second part of the affidavit is the description of the location to be searched. Lee had already gotten the legal description of the property that included the range, township, and section. I added a written description describing the exterior of the property. That sounds simple, but if I got anything such as the color of the roof wrong, Lubinski's attorney would get the warrant quashed along with the evidence.

The third part of the document is the description of the items to be searched for and seized. This too may sound simple, but the Fourth Amendment to the U.S.

Constitution, which is the foundation to all search and seizure law says that the items listed must be *particularly described*. Lube's .22 rifle was easy, but I had to use my imagination on the eagle feather and the photo album. Mike had snuck in and marked the bolt cutters with his initials, so that one was effortless.

The fourth part of a warrant is its body. The legal world calls it the probable cause or "PC" statement. This section must include information that would lead a reasonable person to conclude that there is a "fair probability" the listed items we wanted to search for would be found at the lodge and why they were of evidentiary value in the prosecution of a criminal act. This section has detail about what happened or was said on what date. Had Mike and I not documented everything in our reports, writing the affidavits would have been impossible.

Lee had gone through our reports and had much of the PC written out, but there were areas that needed to be expanded upon and explained so the judge could follow easily and would believe two things; a crime had been committed, and that the evidence was probably going to be found at the lodge. The challenge with this portion of the affidavit wasn't that it was thin; the problem was that we had a tremendous amount of information that needed to be written. After eleven typewritten pages, Lee was satisfied with it.

We piggybacked a lot of the PC from the search warrant affidavit onto the Lubinski arrest warrant and the same for formal complaints that would be served on Jimmy. Lee called the courthouse, and the judge said he would see us at four. I sat in the office while Lee went out and bought us a late lunch. When he returned he brought up what I had said about Orofino.

"You're wrong about this community. These people are the salt of the earth. You've been hobnobbing with the parasites. When this case is over, I want you and Mike to have dinner with my wife and me."

We ate lunch and went over the affidavits for one final polish. Shortly before four o'clock, he left his office to meet with the judge. A few minutes later I walked over to the courthouse as nervous as a mouse in a cathouse. I found Lee in the judge's chambers. He introduced me to the magistrate and the court clerk. I was sworn in, and the judge quietly read through the documents. I took the time to examine his office decor. There were numerous art prints on the wall. They were all pictures of moose. I looked back at the judge as he was reading the search warrant affidavit. His scalp had gotten noticeably redder. Finally, he looked up at Squires, kept his composure over what he had read, and said we had more than enough probable cause and signed the actual warrants.

I thanked the judge and walked to the front door of the courthouse, expecting to bump into a Charbonneau. Lee had kept the warrants and would deliver them to the briefing that was scheduled for 6:00 p.m. at the hatchery. I managed to get in my rig without being seen by anybody whom I had met in the last few months and headed back to the lodge. I was nervous. There were two more people in the loop.

Mike had prepped Lubinski with a contrived story about just the two of us going out to dinner by ourselves. We got in my rig and drove down to the hatchery. We looked the area over carefully for any sign of someone who might recognize us. We drove behind the buildings and hid my rig as best we could.

Mike's boss Roger waved us into an open door. We walked into a room of buzzing uniforms. A dozen Idaho conservation officers were grouped talking to sheriff Nick Albers. Four of his deputies were talking to a couple of BIA tribal officers. Roger opened the meeting and the room hushed. He presented an organized overview of the case and then went into the bloody details and outlined who would be on what team and what they were tasked to do. Raid packets were handed out, and the questions began.

Albers queried me on the layout of the lodge. His SWAT team would consist of the seven-man entry team and two supporting sniper teams. Each sniper team consisted of a spotter and the actual sniper. The snipers would be in place on the hill above the lodge prior to sunup, and their primary responsibility would be to protect the entry team as they made their approach to the lodge. The entry team would not approach the building until Norman was in custody in Missoula. Albers wanted me out of the lodge prior to their entry for my own safety.

I went over the layout of the building. It was what SWAT called an entry nightmare, with two floors and many compartmentalized rooms. I gave him my best guess threat assessment of Lubinski. I'd never really had an indication that he was violent. However, I had never seen him in the mindset of an imminent arrest plus; my gut told me he probably had a weapon stashed. If he got wind of the raid, it was possible he could react in a manner different from what Mike and I had seen. I gave Albers my threat-assessment of Bill, Olivia, and Kristy, and where I thought everyone would be in the building.

The BIA cops wanted to talk to me about the Charbonneau neighborhood. I asked them whether they knew where Jimmy lived, and they glanced at each other and laughed.

"We've been out there twice lately. The last time was because the neighbors had called complaining that he was screwing a dog on the lawn."

It was a crazy story. Something that you couldn't make up but it was clear that these guys had actually been out there on the call. It was something that was so alien that I doubted the reporting caller could have manufactured.

The tribal officers believed Jimmy would not be a problem as long as he hadn't been into the whiskey. What they were concerned with was my new pal, Clinton.

"He moves a lot of dope and hates whites and cops. We've heard rumors that he's got a machine gun too. He'll probably be okay as long as he doesn't think we're hitting his place."

I told them about our trip to Isabella Creek and wished them luck. Mike and I left the hatchery and drove back to the lodge. It now felt like the entire world knew that we were undercovers. And we were headed back to the lodge to spend the night. It seemed like a stupid idea, and I'd found out in the past that if something felt stupid it probably was stupid. I thought about what the tribal cops had said about Jimmy. My mind echoed back to the night of the Swamp Creek deer and Jimmy's question of "who wants the dying quivers?" I thought about that for a second and told Mike what the cops had said. He gave me a queer look and rolled his eyes.

Past Snow's Rock, we talked about the hazard of staying in the lodge. Mike came up with an idea. When it was time to disappear to our rooms, we'd sneak into the teepee and spend the night there. Lube had equipped it with foam pads and sleeping bags. I wasn't excited about slipping into a dirty sleeping bag, but it would be better than being ambushed like two sleeping ducks in our room. If somebody dropped a dime on us, they'd find an empty room.

We walked into the lodge and there was a fresh blood trail coming in from the garage. Rex was looking towards us talking to Bill.

"We had an accident," Rex sniggered, "Bill went out and killed a doe tonight and he cut his nose trying to skin it."

Bill turned around and looked at us. He had a bloody wad of gauze covering his nose. Mike and I chuckled and back-trailed the blood into the garage. A freshly killed closed-season doe was limply hanging from a rafter. They just couldn't quit killing.

The clock was ticking hard. I expected the phone would ring at any minute and burn us. Mike and Norm loaded his truck with coolers filled with frozen elk meat in preparation for the early morning run. When things quieted down, we disappeared into the dark and crept into the teepee. I took my shoes off and stuck my .38 in the shoe closest to my head. I lay down on the foam pad still wearing my clothes. There was no way I was going to strip down. I considered cutting the lodge's phone line but mothballed the idea.

I lay awake listening for the phone to ring inside the lodge. As long as it remained quiet, and no stranger drove up, I knew we would be okay. It was a long, soundless night.

Before light, Mike was up and gone with Norm. I crawled out of the teepee at sunup, smelling of sweat and feeling greasy. I took a pee knowing there were four camouflaged men watching me from the hill. I walked into the quiet lodge—the place was undisturbed, as I expected no one was up. I went to the bedroom and grabbed my towel. I really needed to get out of the place, but I needed a shower. I walked into the bathroom and turned the water on. I pulled my .38 out from under my shirt and placed it in the soap dish. I stripped down and stepped into the warm water and drew the curtain closed. My mind visualized the shower scene from the movie *Psycho* where the gal gets knifed through the curtain and a minute later I was drying myself off. The wet pistol found its place inside my pants, and I quickly went outside, glanced up on the hill, and drove off. Henderson was gone. He'd left the Crabtree for good.

I drove down to the hatchery hoping for some hot coffee and maybe a doughnut. I was surprised to see Jerry Conley, the agency's director, talking to Roger. I sat down with the two of them. They were both energized by the imminent raid. Jerry told me that the first job he had in wildlife was as a game warden in Kansas and he laid out the tale of his first arrest. He said he'd read our reports and was absorbed with what had transpired during the investigation.

Roger turned to me, "We've got information on a guy in Grangeville selling all sorts of wildlife parts out of a pawn shop. When the smoke clears on this case I'd like you to take a look at the file and see if you'd feel like taking a run at him."

The phone rang, and Roger picked it up, listened and turned to me smiling. "They just arrested Norman Charbonneau in Missoula. It went without a hitch and Mike's okay," he turned to a deputy holding a radio mike and nodded.

It was the go-moment for Albers' entry team. Two officers breached Lubinski's bedroom within sixty seconds of going through the front door and had muzzles on the two sleepers before they could lift their heads. "POLICE, DON'T MOVE!" barked through the lodge.

Kristy squealed, stood up naked on the bed, and yelled, "Don't shoot, I'm one of the good guys!"

Lubinski was cuffed without a scuffle.

It was time for me to drive back to the lodge and show the search team where the evidence was located. I slipped a badge necklace on over my head and drove up the grade. I thought about Roger and decided I was probably wrong about his bean-counting mentality. I thought about my upbringing and respect for the laws of the land and how Lubinski and the Charbonneaus had never known such a compass. I thought about Mickey

White's admiration for a trafficker that had murdered two wardens. I flashed on Mickey's girlfriend, now dead with a bullet in her head. I passed Snow's Rock and thought about how this case had changed me. Eight months ago I had been a bit guileless. An innocent. I'd believed that there were a few guys out there that would bend the law, maybe use their wife's tag, however in Lubinski's realm every time Mike and I had turned around we'd met someone else that would try to get away with as much as they could when it came to wildlife. For the rest of my career I would find that if I looked under a few rocks, there would always be another Lubinski or Charbonneau lurking and I was convinced without laws and wardens there would be no wildlife.

I drove into the lodge's driveway and parked. Rex Lubinski stared out from the passenger side of a deputy's SUV. His arms were handcuffed behind his back causing him to lean forward. He gaped at me through the window as I stepped from my vehicle, he gave me a baffled look and then his clenched jaw slumped—he knew.

Two conservation officers were talking to Kristy. I walked over to her and she stared at the badge on my chest. I told her that I was not Tony Henderson and that *I was a game warden.*

She looked up into my eyes, mentally bankrupt and asked, "Does this mean you won't be staying for dinner?"

Epilogue

Rex Lubinski

Rex Lubinski was arrested on September 3, 1992, and was charged with 32 counts. All were misdemeanors except one felony of aiding and abetting a burglary. Seven days later Lubinski posted bond and was released from the Clearwater County Jail.

Lubinski was facing a costly extended trial that would also incur a large expenditure for Clearwater County. The reality of our criminal justice system is that it simply doesn't have the resources to take every accused person to trial who enters a plea of not guilty—nor should it. It operates on what is called judicial economy. The judicial system has three options with any criminal proceeding: drop the charges, go to trial, or reach a plea agreement. The case against Lubinski was like cured concrete. Lubinski had no wiggle space. It was time for him to deal. In reality, it didn't matter whether he went down on all the charges or half of them. The judge had plenty of sentencing leeway and Lubinski was going to receive a harsh penalty.

Squires discussed a proposed plea agreement with Mike and me. We were comfortable with dismissing all, but seventeen of the counts.

Lubinski agreed to change his plea to guilty on the seventeen. He and his attorney would argue for mercy while Squires would articulate why Lubinski deserved something more fitting for his crimes.

Mike and I testified at Lubinski's sentencing in
Orofino. The assigned magistrate was Patrick Costello. It
was a curious atmosphere since I hadn't seen Lubinski
since his arrest—and hadn't talked to him as an officer.
Just prior to the hearing, Rex noticed me outside the
courtroom and walked over. "Tony," he said smiling.
"Whadda been up to?"

I was stunned. He was acting as though I was still his
old buddy. I paused, looked him in the eye, and gave him
a biting answer. "The usual, Rex, chasing crooks." His
shoulders slumped, and he rejoined his attorney. I think
I hurt his feelings.

The sentencing took most of the day. Part of the
process involved showing the judge two freezers full of
meat that were in pickup trucks guarded by uniformed
conservation officers outside the courthouse. Although
court was still in session, it was a much less formal
atmosphere than in the courtroom. While Judge Costello
was examining the freezer contents, Lubinski opened his
mouth. "Maybe we should try some smoked steelhead,
your honor," he said it with a snicker.

I don't think Rex was serious. I think it was just a
stupid good-ol'-boy remark that backfired and resulted
in a nasty glare from the judge.

Judge Costello fined Lubinski $4,850 and assessed
an additional civil penalty of $2,700. Most of the civil
assessment was for two moose that Lubinski had
unlawfully possessed. With additional $680 in court
costs, it totaled $8,230. Costello revoked his hunting
privileges for seventeen years and remanded him to the
custody of the Clearwater County jail for 180 days with

an additional 210 days hanging over his head—pending his conduct during two years of probation. It was rewarding to see Rex Lubinski cuffed by a deputy and hauled to jail.

That night, Lubinski complained of chest pains to his jailer and they rushed him to the emergency room. I don't know what the diagnosis was, but I'm highly suspicious of the event. Lubinski was released from jail on a medical furlough.

His release set in motion a long court battle led by Lee Squires. Lubinski claimed he couldn't go back to jail because he needed exercise to maintain his health. Mike and I wrote up affidavits stating that we had never witnessed the man exercising. Arguments for and against his incarceration were heard before Judge Costello on December 28, 1993. The judge ordered him back to jail starting on January 4th.

In March of 1996 warden Matt Erickson charged Lubinski with "purchasing a hunting license while revoked." He entered a not guilty plea and acted as his own attorney. He explained to the jury that the computer system allowed him to purchase the license, and thus it wasn't his fault. The jury didn't buy his innocence and declared him guilty. The judge fined him $561 and added another year to his revocation. After a year of not paying his fine, the judge issued a bench warrant and he was arrested for failure to pay.

Jimmy Charbonneau

The Clearwater County Prosecutor's Office charged Jimmy with seven misdemeanor wildlife counts. The Missoula County Prosecutor charged him with one count of felony sale of wildlife and had him arrested and extradited to Montana. The U.S. Attorney's office charged him with sexual assault.

Charbonneau entered a guilty plea and was sentence to the federal penitentiary for 27 months for the sexual crime against Trudy.

Prosecutor John Swain promised he'd prosecute Charbonneau on the state charges when he was released but dismissed all counts on June 29, 1993. I haven't added up how much money we paid Charbonneau for the meat, but he walked away with it when the charges were dumped.

On May 15, 1993 Idaho Fish and Game received a letter from the Nez Perce Tribal Prosecutor. The letter stated that they had charged Jimmy Charbonneau with 14 counts stemming from our investigation and promised to prosecute him pending his release from federal custody. While researching this book, I sent a letter to the tribal court requesting the disposition of the case but unfortunately they did not respond. I'd like to believe that retribution for the crimes Charbonneau committed against the Clearwater's wildlife was delivered by the tribe. Unfortunately it's quite possible the charges were dropped for reasons of judicial economy.

The Missoula County court sentenced him to three years in the state penitentiary, but suspended his sentence to "time served," which was at least 90 days. He was placed on probation for three years. The judge also ordered him to reimburse Montana for the money he'd received from Gary Burke. As part of his sentencing, he was ordered to perform 100 hours of community service. The Dworshak Hatchery agreed to take Jimmy on for his community service time after his release from the federal penitentiary. In a letter addressed to the court, Facility Manager Bill Miller wrote about Charbonneau's efforts and that "he had a good attitude and never complained."

On December 3, 2000, Deputy Rex Summerfield caught Charbonneau with two elk on private property outside the reservation boundaries. Since private property isn't "unclaimed land," as per the treaty, the elk were killed "closed-season" and thus illegal. Summerfield seized the elk and charged him with two counts. In a plea deal, Charbonneau agreed to enter a guilty plea to one count and the other one was dropped. Judge Randall Robinson fined him $110.

Norman Charbonneau

Norman was arrested at gunpoint in Missoula on September 3, 1992 by Montana Fish, Wildlife, & Parks' buy-bust arrest team and was charged with two felony counts of sale of wildlife. He entered a not guilty plea and sat in the county jail until December 10th, when he changed his plea to guilty.

The judge sentenced him to three years in the penitentiary but suspended all, but the time served. He was ordered to pay back the money Burke had paid him for the elk and to perform 100 hours of community service during his three-year probation.

On May 12, 1993, the Nez Perce Tribal Court found Norman Charbonneau guilty of eight charges stemming from our investigation. The court fined him $1,175 and took his tribal hunting and fishing privileges away for twelve years. This was a genuine eye-opener for me. The tribe had a reputation for not enforcing its wildlife laws at the time of this investigation. It makes me believe that we should have worked with the tribe during the prosecution phase of this investigation.

In 1994 Norman violated his Montana probation. I was unable to determine what he actually did to cause this action. He was arrested and hauled back up the Lochsa River to Missoula. Judge Edward McLean sent him to Deer Lodge State Prison for two and a half years.

On August 28, 1998, Norman was charged by warden Tanna Ragen for unlawful possession of an elk. He failed to appear for his trial, was arrested, fined $1,000 and spent nine days in jail. He agreed to a deferred payment schedule, but failed to make his agreed payments. A warrant was issued for his arrest for failure to pay on January 10, 2000. It was never served on him. He must have gone on the lam. Norman Charbonneau died in 2010. His obituary didn't mention a cause of death.

Tom Charbonneau

We had one good count against Tom for the sale of the smoked steelhead he had stolen from his father. For whatever reason, he was never charged for it although the exchange of money took place outside the reservation. I have no idea what happened when his father found out that he and Jimmy had stolen his stash at the church. I have to assume that Basil didn't let it slide off his back.

In November, 1994 warden Kevin Olson caught Tom with an illegal elk. He was fined and never paid. Warrants were issued twice for failure to pay. He set up a deferred payment plan with the court on August 12, 1996. Twenty-nine days later he was killed when he drove his car into the Clearwater River. It was determined that alcohol was a factor that contributed to the accident.

At the time of his death, Tom had met a newcomer to Ahsahka that was living next to the Woodlot. The two had plans to hunt together. His new acquaintance was undercover game warden Paul Loveall.

I still feel empathy for Tom Charbonneau.

Newt Isaac

Newt Isaac was never charged by the county for his sale of steelhead since everything occurred within the reservation boundaries. The case was turned over to the Nez Perce Tribe, Office of the Prosecutor, but

unfortunately the one-year statute of limitations had run
its course.

In October 2011, I found him with a Google search
listed as an inmate at the Lewiston-Clarkston Valley Jails
for an undetermined crime. He's currently listed as a
registered sex offender living in Kamiah resulting from
"unlawful sexual intercourse." It's too bad he didn't stick
with magazines.

Jerry and Larry Lubinski

Both were charged with the unlawful killing of elk
and hunting without licenses. Neither appeared on the
charges. Arrest warrants were issued for failure to
appear. Since the violations were misdemeanors, there
was no possibility of extradition.

Today, there is the Interstate Violators Compact with
37 states that have passed legislation joining the
compact. The compact's purpose is to address the
problem of wildlife criminals moving across state lines
and avoiding justice in the process. If the Lubinskis
committed their crimes today, the two would lose their
hunting privileges in all 37 states, including Idaho and
their home state of Wisconsin—until they faced justice.

Basil Charbonneau

In June 1993, warden Mark Hill caught Basil Charbonneau selling salmon. He failed to appear, and was arrested, and eventually, entered a guilty plea.

In 2001, Basil raped a 72 year-old-woman. He was charged with aggravated sexual assault and entered a guilty plea to a lesser charge in 2003. He was sentenced to 48 months. The government filed a motion with the court under the Adam Walsh Act to declare Charbonneau a "sexually dangerous person" for a permanent commitment. His court appointed attorney successfully argued for his release. He's now a registered sex offender living in Lewiston.

Mickey White

Mickey is doing life plus 14 years in the Idaho State Penitentiary for murder. I don't think he'll escape.

Ahsahka Nez Perce Presbyterian Church

On Christmas Eve 2008, members of the church were preparing dinner in the building that the Charbonneaus had burglarized. A fire started in the main church, and the 118 year old structure burned nearly to the ground. It was rebuilt the following year.

Sale of Fish by Nez Perce Tribal Members

Sometime after this investigation the tribe loosened its laws pertaining to the sale of fish. The sale of steelhead and salmon by tribal members is now legal. When this happened, I recoiled. It was contrary to my core belief concerning the commercialization of wildlife. However, I must recall the history of the Clearwater. Two hundred years ago the Nez Perce chose to sell salmon to Lewis and Clark's Corps of Discovery and without this assistance they might not have made it. I still don't agree with the tribe's decision but urge the reader to make up his or her own mind on the issue.

Stronger Idaho Wildlife Laws

In the late winter of 1992, Governor Cecil D. Andrus signed into law legislation that made most of the crimes Rex Lubinski had committed felonies. Unfortunately, it didn't become law until July 1st, 1992. Had the law taken effect a year earlier, Lubinski probably would have exhibited "chest pains" in prison.

Additional laws were passed in Idaho in 1997 that increased the statute of limitations on wildlife crimes and allowed the courts to take away violators' hunting privileges, under certain circumstances for life. I'm certain that Rex Lubinski would have been an excellent candidate for a lifetime revocation had Judge Costello had this option at the time of his sentencing.

Mike Best aka Peyton Parker

Mike continued to work in Idaho's Special Investigations Unit for nine years. In 1994, Mike successfully investigated three groups of traffickers in the Salmon area. I gave him behind-the-scenes support along with taking on the post-raid overt investigation. As expected he was a pleasure to work with. In 1995 he was awarded Idaho Fish and Game's Officer of the Year award for his numerous accomplishments while working undercover. He received the award at the department's in-service banquet while wearing a gorilla suit to protect his identity.

Tony Latham aka Tony Henderson

A year after the Crabtree case, Mike talked me into taking on a solo undercover case in Grangeville. The perpetrator was trafficking in wildlife parts from all over the world. The operation was unexpectedly terminated when the target and his wife were tortured to death in their home. A year later I commenced a covert case in Orofino involving an unlicensed outfitter that was laundering illegal mountain lion hunts through his taxidermy business. I wasn't excited about taking it on since I was concerned with getting burned by someone from the previous case. After four years, the case was successfully prosecuted in federal court based on a violation of the federal Lacey Act–moving illegal wildlife across state lines.

Throughout my years as an Idaho game warden I continued with undercover work from time to time and would not have considered my career complete without the experience.

Bill Snow's Rock

The rock is still there. Bill told me that a lady had called him and asked him whether he would mind if she painted over the offensive inscription since it was on a school bus route. Bill endorsed the idea, and the rock was painted. He tells me the inscription is starting to show through.

Acknowledgements

First to Gary Burke and Mike Best. This tale (and the
justice that followed) wouldn't have happened without
their expertise in undercover work. I can't leave out
Jerry Conley, the director of Idaho Fish and Game from
1980 through 1996. The department's Special
Investigations Unit would have withered on the vine
without Jerry's belief in covert investigations.

During a homicide investigation, detectives put
together something called the *murder book* that is
bound by at least one four-inch binder. Long-term
undercover wildlife investigations produce something
similar but usually more voluminous. In my mind, I
always referred to the case binders produced during
these investigations as the murder book. I believe it's a
proper term. Since this case transpired twenty years ago,
I needed its murder book to cut through the fog of my
memory. Fortunately, Idaho Fish and Game still had the
original document boxes archived away. Through an
open records request I received a copy that was just
short of a thousand pages. Chris Wright, Nancy Swain,
and Lori Lyman of the enforcement bureau went through
the hundreds of pages, copied them off, and blacked out
personal information about people who hadn't been
charged. I'm certain the trio spent weeks on my request.

My sister, Jane Griffith, edited these pages. It took
me eighty-four days to write the draft of this thing–I
believe it may take longer to edit a book than it does to
write one. Without her red pen, this book would have

been a disaster. Her husband, Jay Griffith designed the cover and read the manuscript for content.

Thanks to all! - Tony H. Latham

<<<<>>>>

Made in the USA
Lexington, KY
14 October 2012